More Praise for *The Greater Goal*

"I believe passionately in the principles of the *Greater Goal*. We are putting them to work for us right now in my organization."
— **Janet A. Tobian, MD, PhD, Senior Medical Director and Global Brand Development Leader, Eli Lilly and Company**

"My friends Ken and Heather have created a remarkable book that will help you put servant leadership to work. Bravo!"
— **Dr. Kent M. Keith, CEO, Greenleaf Center for Servant Leadership**

"Health care is a cause that most people join for higher reasons than just to make a living. So *The Greater Goal*, with its fresh and challenging style, will have particular relevance for the healthcare sector."
— **Dr. Richard Barker, author of *2030: The Future of Medicine***

"There is no greater goal than service; Ken and Heather's latest book serves us all. Every aerospace company I know can use it!"
— **Dr. Kees Rietsema (USAF Col., Ret.) Chair, Department of Business Administration, Embry-Riddle Aeronautical University Worldwide**

"Ken and Heather point the way to connecting life purpose and the achievement of greater goals. The authors' approach can heal the brokenness of our leaders and organizations today."
— **Father Bill Brown, Director, St. Joseph's Retreat House**

"My professional life has revolved around conveying a compelling story about the greater purpose of organizations. *The Greater Goal* helps you to do just that—and more."
— **Andrea V. Cotter, Senior Vice President and Chief Communications Officer**

"*The Greater Goal* will give leaders at every level practical advice on setting and achieving meaningful goals together."
— **Douglas D, Hawthorne, FACHE, CEO, Texas Health Resources**

"Strategic alignment is crucial to large multihospital systems. The five practices of Greater Goal achievement help us do just that!"
— **Paul N. Patton, Vice President, Human Resources, Yale–New Haven Hospital**

"I love what Ken and Heather are saying in *The Greater Goal*. I intend to buy two dozen books and give copies to friends and clients."
  —Hank Higdon, Founding Partner, HigdonBraddockMatthews LLC

"Aligning everyone's actions in executing the Greater Goal isn't as easy as it sounds. Here's the game plan you need to make it happen."
  —Lt. Gen. Robert E. Kelley, USAF, Ret.

"How can my work have meaning? My friends Ken and Heather answer that question by taking you on an adventure in pursuit of meaning and achievement. I highly recommend this engaging book."
  —Gary W. Moon, PhD, Executive Director, Martin Family Institute and Dallas Willard Center, Westmont College

"The unprecedented complexity in today's marketplace requires leadership that is conspicuous in its pursuit of what matters. The authors have shared the straightforward path toward achieving competitive advantage. Start-ups and multinationals alike will, no doubt, take heed of what this book reveals."
  —Deb Lantz, Executive Director, Marketing and Communications, Tepper School of Business, Carnegie Mellon University

"*The Greater Goal* is aimed right at the heart of this generation of leaders. Ken and Heather show us how to do both good and great things!"
  —Ginger Graham, Senior Lecturer, Harvard University, and CEO coach

"*The Greater Goal* touched me deeply. It will guide you to improving your business results and the quality of your life. I've applied these principles to my company and my personal life with tremendous results in both."
  —Michael Holmes, President, Rx Outreach, Inc.

"The tools in *The Greater Goal* have changed the way we approach our strategy and the way we do our work. I highly recommend it!"
  —Newt Crenshaw, Vice President, Oncology Business Unit, Eli Lilly and Company

"I am a strong believer in the power of being purposeful. I really appreciated the careful thought and wisdom I found in *The Greater Goal*. It's an insightful and effective framework for the achievement of shared goals."
  —Mark M. Ferrara, Vice President, Talent Management, Eli Lilly and Company

THE
GREATER
GOAL

Other Books by Ken Jennings

(with John Stahl-Wert)

The Serving Leader

Ten Thousand Horses

THE
GREATER
GAL

CONNECTING PURPOSE
AND PERFORMANCE

KEN JENNINGS
AND HEATHER HYDE

BK

Berrett–Koehler Publishers, Inc.
San Francisco
a BK Business book

Berrett-Koehler Publishers, Inc.
1333 Broadway, Suite 1000
Oakland, CA 94612-1921
Tel: (510) 817-2277   Fax: (510) 817-2278   www.bkconnection.com

Ordering Information
Quantity sales. Special discounts are available on quantity purchases by corporations, associations, and others. For details, contact the "Special Sales Department" at the Berrett-Koehler address above.
Individual sales. Berrett-Koehler publications are available through most bookstores. They can also be ordered directly from Berrett-Koehler:
Tel: (800) 929-2929; Fax: (802) 864-7626; www.bkconnection.com
Orders for college textbook/course adoption use. Please contact Berrett-Koehler:
Tel: (800) 929-2929; Fax: (802) 864-7626.
Orders by U.S. trade bookstores and wholesalers. Please contact Ingram Publisher Services, Tel: (800) 509-4887; Fax: (800) 838-1149; E-mail: customer .service@ingrampublisherservices.com; or visit www.ingrampublisherservices.com /Ordering for details about electronic ordering.

Berrett-Koehler and the BK logo are registered trademarks of Berrett-Koehler Publishers, Inc.

Printed in the United States of America

Berrett-Koehler books are printed on long-lasting acid-free paper. When it is available, we choose paper that has been manufactured by environmentally responsible processes. These may include using trees grown in sustainable forests, incorporating recycled paper, minimizing chlorine in bleaching, or recycling the energy produced at the paper mill.

Library of Congress Cataloging-in-Publication Data
Jennings, Ken (Kenneth R.)
  The greater goal : connecting purpose and performance / Ken Jennings and Heather Hyde.
     p. cm.
  ISBN 978-1-60994-288-5 (pbk.)
  1. Leadership. 2. Goal (Psychology) 3. Strategy. 4. Motivation (Psychology) 5. Organizational effectiveness. I. Hyde, Heather. II. Title.
  HD57.7.J457 2012
  658.4—dc23   2011042147

FIRST EDITION
20 19 18 17 16   10 9 8 7 6 5 4 3

Cover design: Cassandra Chu
Interior design and composition: Beverly Butterfield, Girl of the West Productions
Editing: PeopleSpeak

To our parents, thanks for showing us
how to live and love well

To our children, each with a
special story yet to tell

To each other, we are dedicated

To our readers and all who seek Greater Goals

Do all the good you can
by all the means you can,
in all the ways you can,
in all the places you can,
at all the times you can,
to all the people you can,
as long as ever you can
—John Wesley

Contents

Foreword by
Ken Blanchard

I have found that over the years, without a Greater Goal to serve, the only thing people have to serve is themselves—and we have all seen the negative effect of self-serving leadership in every segment of our society. That's why I'm excited about this book.

Wouldn't you love to come home from work every night knowing that you gave your very best for a worthy cause? How would it be if you shared in setting the most important goals at work, even if you're not the company president? And what would it be like if you knew exactly how your efforts at work were part of creating a community capable of outstanding performance? My friends Ken Jennings and Heather Hyde invite you to imagine your work life this way as they show you what it takes to create high performance based on high purpose. Welcome to *The Greater Goal: Connecting Purpose and Performance*, a wonderful expedition into how people, teams, and organizations create shared purpose for the greater good *and* achieve outstanding organizational results. It's a story, a road map, and a journey with a very special purpose.

For over a decade my colleagues and I have been speaking about how organizational high performance is achieved by focusing on the "triple bottom line"—being the employer of choice, the provider of choice, and the investment of choice. Over time, we learned that high-performing organizations have leadership that influences people by unleashing their power and potential to impact the greater good. But it's not just about setting and achieving more and more difficult goals. Leaders who can create, with others, the organization's shared Greater Goal *and* show how people can align their best efforts to it show the way to high performance.

Ken and Heather have chosen to illustrate the power of having a Greater Goal through the story of Alex Beckley, your average troubled leader. I love the business fable format, and I believe readers do too—especially when they get a new insight into a simple, time-tested truth. Books like the one you are holding can cut straight to the heart of how you think and feel about life at work by tapping into your own truth—your experiences, memories, perceptions—while at the same time offering new ways of seeing. Stories like this allow readers to suspend their skepticism and consider the power of personal narrative. Those of us who have been around the block a time or two know that our narratives become so deeply rooted that they can run our lives—even determine our destiny.

In *The Greater Goal*, Ken and Heather invite you to listen to one leader's story and to look at your own. The facts and figures of your accomplishments are not the whole picture. Wherever we contribute in our organizations and communities, each of us leaves behind a legacy—a story of what's possible. This book encourages you to form your legacy around a Greater Goal and connect your high purpose with high performance.

Imagine that life's most stubborn obstacles—the reasons why you fall short of your potential for greater good—can be left behind with the next decision you make. You don't need to have a life-threatening wake-up call (like the hero of this tale) to give yourself a second chance. Transformational change can also take place in the small, everyday choices we make.

Seeking the greater good, and seeking it together, is truly a worthy Greater Goal.

Ken Blanchard
January 2012

Introduction

In this new book, the coauthor of the bestselling *The Serving Leader* provides a road map that all leaders can use to create top performance by aligning the entire organization, at all levels, with the higher purposes of the organization.

Ken Jennings teams with his longtime collaborator Heather Hyde to provide an inspiring and practical guide to succeeding at today's top leadership priorities:

- Articulating the higher purposes of organizations
- Creating shared goals among all stakeholders
- Aligning all functions around the shared goals and higher purposes
- Driving higher organizational performance

Like *The Serving Leader*, this new book is a short, easy-to-read narrative that offers powerful ideas and practical strategies through an engaging fictional story. It is the story of Alex Beckley, the new president of a medical products company, who receives a wake-up call that inspires him to live and lead

1

differently. Alex learns the Star Model of high purpose and high performance and uses this model to change his strategies and behavior and thereby dramatically raise his leadership effectiveness and the performance of his organization.

Please join us for a look inside the Star Model and experience how alignment to your Greater Goals will unleash one of the most powerful forces on earth.

A Greater Goal has three specific dimensions. First, the goal is great in the sense that it aims for a greater good—hugely positive outcomes for many. Second, it is great because it requires the combined and aligned best efforts of everyone in the whole company. And third, it calls each of us individually to greatness, to give our very best and to become part of something greater than ourselves.

An organization aligned, individual-by-individual and team-by-team, to a shared Greater Goal is one of the most powerful forces for good on earth.

1. Hard Drive

At 5:30 a.m., with late summer thunder rumbling in his ears, Alexander Beckley slumped in his chair, staring at his computer screen. Every now and then, lightning flickered across his face. The monitor glowed in the dark, highlighting the divot in Alex's nose—a souvenir of his college boxing career. Another flash of lightning revealed the worry lines and a little gray in his short blond hair. Alex didn't blink. His head felt hot, his stomach felt cold, and his heart was somewhere north of his Adam's apple. All he could see were the words glaring back at him:

From:	Dan Meyers [mailto:dmeyers@beckleymedical.com]
Sent:	Tuesday, April 19, 2011 11:52 PM
To:	Alex Beckley [mailto: abeckley@beckleymedical.com]
Subject:	Board meeting follow-up

Alex,

Hearing strong feedback from the board on last night's call.

They know you are working hard, but frustration levels are rising.

Call me to talk.

It was signed by the board chair and acting CEO, Dan Myers. Alex knew he was now in danger of losing the support of the company his father had founded. *I will fail him even in this*, he thought, watching light flash across the room.

With a click of his mouse, Alex switched screens from his e-mail to his schedule. If he could close the deal for the company's new line of products with University Health System, it would be the company's biggest deal ever, and maybe that would impress the board enough to forget about his recent poor performance. Today he was back in selling mode, showing University Health that his company, Beckley Medical Products, was the perfect partner. UHS was huge and strategically influential in this town. Today Beckley's president himself would win the work and show his critics the talent they would lose if they let him go.

Alex moved around his house like he moved around life— fast. As he dressed for the day, he reviewed what he knew of UHS, a complex integrated healthcare delivery system and the largest employer in the region. He mentally ticked through his presentation, reciting his sales pitch. He would run through it again in the conference room before anyone else arrived.

The meeting was downtown, and if he didn't want to be stuck in tunnel traffic he would have to take Bigelow Boulevard, a shortcut that would shoot him out right next to the old U.S. Steel Building. The monolithic black structure ruled the Pittsburgh skyline and housed the captains of Pittsburgh's steel industry. Now those offices were also occupied by the administration of UHS—one of the largest health systems in the world. But people still called the building "the Steel Tower."

Just before he closed his calendar, Alex saw the small note in his evening agenda: "Rachel: Hunter-Jumper Competition." He sighed, knowing he wouldn't make it to his daughter's contest once again. As he passed through the kitchen on his way to the car, he found his mother, Annie, and his daughter, Rachel, at the kitchen table. They were watching an early-morning news show with the volume low. His mother still wore the same style housecoat she wore when he was a kid.

"You're up early," she said when he appeared.

"You too," he replied. "Storm wake you up?" he asked Rachel.

She nodded. "It sounded like the tree outside my window exploded."

He kissed the tops of their heads. "Well," he said, "I'm off."

"You don't want any coffee?" his mother asked as Alex pulled on his raincoat. He could hear the torrents coming down outside.

"No, thanks, Mom," he said, fastening the buttons quickly and adjusting his sleeves.

Rachel watched him with a worried look. "Sure hope the weather clears up before tonight. You remember that I am riding tonight, Dad . . . You'll be there, right?"

"I have a long day and a dinner meeting, Rach," he said, avoiding her eyes by fumbling unnecessarily with his coat collar. "I don't think I'll be there. I'm sorry, sweetie. But you and Grandma can tell me all about it later."

Rachel's eyes misted over with an expression of hurt and then resignation that became a frozen stare at the television. His mother's lips pursed and her eyes narrowed. "You work very hard, Alex. Just like your father."

"No, Mom," he said, "not just like him." *For one thing,
I'm not succeeding like Dad did,* he thought. The comment
touched Alex's sore memory of never quite getting enough of
his father's attention to confirm that he measured up. Without
waiting for a reply, Alex vanished out the back door into the
rain. He didn't like disappointing Rachel yet again, but he
didn't see how he had a choice. He was irritated that his
mother compared him to his father. Of all people, she should
know that he wasn't like *him.* Surely she could see he wanted
to give more of himself to the family, even if he couldn't find
the time.

It was true that Alex wanted to be successful—like his
father—but he wanted to do it his way. In the back of his head,
though, a little voice nagged that he *was* just like his father.
He didn't have time for his kid either. Alex was disappointing
Rachel, and her face this morning told him that he was,
indeed, acting just like his old man. But didn't his father have
pressure from his company's board of directors and major
sales to make too?

He sat in his car for a minute before starting it. How did he
get here, back in his boyhood home with his mother and back
at the company his father had built?

Alex left Pittsburgh after grad school to get far away from
the family business—to make a name for himself, on his own,
and in his own style. Growing up as the son of a busy and
driven entrepreneur left an enduring image of what it meant
to be successful and how to get there. Time and distance from
his father did not result in Alex's being any less driven or busy
than his dad, Russ Beckley, had been. Alex's way was full of
drive and determination, and those qualities had gotten him
the recognition he wanted. In the fifteen years he spent away

from Pittsburgh, he had become the executive vice president of a successful company and was on the verge of taking the top position with a firm that competed with his dad's company.

But then, while he was busy making other plans, "life happened." His father sickened and passed away from an aggressive illness, coincidentally on Alex's birthday, forever changing how he would feel on that day. Alex never really got to say good-bye or to sort out his deep feelings for his dad. Just as unexpectedly, the board of Russ Beckley's firm recruited Alex back home to Pittsburgh to take the number-two spot—president—at Beckley. He took the job, reporting to the CEO, Dan Myers, his dad's oldest friend. Dan was seventy years old and would not stay in the CEO role for much longer. That top job *could* be Alex's. But so far, in the two years since he had come on board, the company was not exactly following his lead. Competition in the industry was fierce, Beckley's product innovation had slowed down, some of the company's better talent was restless, and a few recent hires had quit unexpectedly. If Alex didn't figure out how to fix the company soon, he would not succeed his father as CEO.

Alex shook his doubtful circumstances out of his head. Through glimpses of clarity between the rapidly swishing windshield wipers, he navigated across Pittsburgh's wet, hilly backbone. The storm was not letting up. His front right wheel hit a pothole covered by rainwater, and the impact tugged the steering wheel out of his fingers. He cringed. The tires wobbled. Alex groaned. *Hopefully the car was just thrown out of alignment. Not too serious.*

His black BMW sprayed water out from both sides like a speedboat. The rain was heavy now, and through its curtain he could barely see the Pittsburgh skyline ahead. The city teemed with education, medicine, and new high-tech companies. And Beckley was a player on the scene, at least for the moment.

Alex knew in his heart that it had been right to come to Beckley. His wife had died during the same year as his dad, setting up the worst period of his life. Rachel was now approaching twelve years old. She was with her grandmother, and his mother was not alone. Faced with all of the life changes he could not control, he thought at least running Beckley would be in his power. But in the two years since he had returned to Pittsburgh and Beckley Medical, it seemed that his aggressive style of bottom-line, results-driven leadership was making things worse.

But today was a new day. He would be the hero, the super sales rep, and close this deal with UHS. His belt began to buzz as his BlackBerry vibrated with a message. He fiddled with the magnetic strap that held the phone in place and tapped the e-mail icon. It was from Nate Strayer, Beckley's chief financial officer. He shifted his eyes from the road to the message.

HOOOOOONNNNK!!!!!!

Adrenaline bolted through his body as he looked up. He had drifted out of his lane and was cutting off a truck behind him. Alex jammed his steering wheel over, a hard left—so hard he hit the divider in the middle of the road. His car bounced sideways, the wheels caught and tripped, and the car flipped. He was tumbling over and over until even the stout BMW roof began to crumple, straining against physics to protect its driver. Windows cracked into a thousand shards but held together like sparkling sheets. Something large hit Alex in the chest, and as the car came to rest upside down, he could barely breathe. Smoke from the airbags billowed around him, filling his lungs with a burning sensation.

"Please, God," he choked, "don't let me die." He didn't recognize his words. His voice sounded strange to his ringing ears. Fumbling for the seat belt, he found he couldn't move his arms, and even if he could, he was hanging upside down. Or maybe he was pinned against the steering wheel—he wasn't sure. He couldn't feel anything, or at least anything he recognized. "God," he said again, "help me?"

Immediately, he heard a voice. It didn't sound like God.

"He's alive!" Alex heard someone say.

"Hey, buddy," said another voice. A hand touched his shoulder. Alex saw a blurry, bearded face, inches from his own, from which came the words "Buddy, you're gonna be alright. They're already comin' to get you. You hang tough." Then he heard the same voice mutter to someone, "I guess all he can really *do* is hang."

Another voice from further away said, "That guy is messed *up!*"

"God," Alex groaned for the last time. As he descended into welcome unconsciousness, he heard the sirens. This was not how he was supposed to get to UHS.

When Alex opened his eyes again, all he saw was white. *Am I dead?* No answer. *Yup, I'm dead.* But even as he wondered, machines and tubes started coming into focus in front of him. And then they were gone as he slipped back into unconsciousness.

Over the next few days, Alex was in and out of awareness—
and pain. Sometimes he came to and felt as if he were float-
ing. At other points he came to and felt excruciating pressure.

Rachel was there each time he awoke. Sitting next to his
bed, she looked so much like her mother with the little worry
line in the middle of her forehead. Her chocolate-brown hair
was always falling haphazardly out of her ponytail. *Rachel.* He
didn't notice when he started saying her name out loud.

"Daddy?" The sweet, anxious face appeared closer. "I'm
right here, Dad."

Then she was gone. When she came back, he found he
could say more than one word this time.

"Hey, Dad," she said.

Alex thought she looked like an angel. "Hey, sweetie," he
said. "How long?"

"You've been out for a few days, Dad. You had surgery. I
was scared."

Alex smiled weakly.

Rachel's eyebrows squeezed a line of worry between them.
"They're gonna keep you here for a while. The doctor said
it could have been worse—and you should see the car!" She
sighed and smiled at Alex. "I'm so glad you're alive, Dad. You
are all I have."

Rachel touched her father's forearm, careful not to disturb
the IV tubing taped there. "You know I said I would never
come into a hospital again, not after Mom."

Alex heard only half of what she said. Stronger than one of
those dreams that he sometimes remembered in the middle
of the day, Alex saw the accident flying through his mind with
crystal-clear vision. He remembered the storm, the truck, the
BlackBerry—and the appointment at UHS.

"I . . . I . . . remember," he said, his eyes staring at the ceiling. "I had a meeting and . . . my phone. Where's my phone? I need my phone," Alex said urgently.

Rachel stared at him, her mouth dropping open. A sickness in her stomach became a darkness in her face. "Your BlackBerry? You want your phone?"

"I need to call, to find out, to reschedule . . . "

Her eyes filled with tears. "You're really screwed up, Dad." She wiped the tears on her sleeve. "You just care about work." She wiped her eyes again and picked up her backpack. "I'll see you later, Dad."

"Rachel, I . . . " He couldn't follow.

A nurse walked in and picked up his chart. "We're awake, are we, Mr. Beckley?" She glanced at a machine and wrote something on the chart. "How do you feel?"

"Hurts," Alex said, staring at the chair where Rachel had been sitting.

The nurse injected something into his IV. It wasn't long before Alex didn't feel anything at all.

Alex's next visitor was Kevin Jordan, his chief operating officer. Kevin was a former professional football player, and he looked like he belonged in a uniform rather than his business suit. When Alex came around, Kevin was standing at the foot of his bed smiling—the creases in his skin seemed to wrap around his shaved head.

"I see that you did make it to a UHS hospital after all. Nice work. But you are now officially on the injured reserve list."

Alex grinned. "Funny, Kevin. I'm glad you're here." In his transition to leading Beckley Medical, Kevin had been his main guide. But Kevin often disagreed with Alex's approach to leading the company, saying things like, "That's not the way things work here." Still, Kevin did his best to help Alex, and the two had become friends of sorts.

Kevin told Alex that his responsibilities had been delegated. Even so, he had brought with him a new cell phone for Alex, a shining new BlackBerry, all programmed and ready to go. "Use this carefully," he joked.

Then his tone became serious. "You know, Alex, you are going to have to come back slowly." He paused. "Dan and I have been talking. Don't worry—I wasn't going over your head. We have a suggestion."

Alex felt both confused and apprehensive. "Go on."

"Dan and I have a good friend who is also a consultant. Well, he's more than that. He used to be one of your dad's key advisors. We got to know him during the time you were working back east, so you missed meeting him."

Alex stiffened. He didn't need a consultant. *Probably some old-school guy who quotes business-school case studies.* Kevin waited quietly as minutes went by. Alex thought of his performance struggles at work and of Rachel stomping out. He supposed he should take the offer of help with the business and wondered how he would ever improve life at home. Alex nodded. "Call him for me? I guess I could use the help. Thank you, Kevin."

Kevin picked up Alex's new phone to call Quinn McDougall. He hit the speakerphone button. Alex noticed that Kevin smiled as he heard Quinn's voice. It was a happy voice—and maybe Scottish? Alex wasn't sure.

"Quinn," Kevin said, "Meet my boss, Alex. He's Russ Beckley's son, you know."

The accented voice over the speakerphone said, "It's a pleasure to meet you, Alex. Your father told me so much about your accomplishments. He was proud. How can I help?"

Alex replayed his accident and reported the board's unhappiness, and he even mentioned his concern about his daughter. Unexpected words poured out of Alex. Kevin took his leave. When he had concluded his emotional monologue, Alex paused to say, "Do you think you could help me?"

Quinn let the silence linger for a moment. "Perhaps," he replied slowly, suggesting more was left unsaid. "Why don't we get together and discuss it?"

"You will have to come to me," Alex said, looking at his leg cast.

"Sure," Quinn said. "In the meantime, I'd like you to consider exactly what you will do with this second chance."

When Kevin left the hospital, he drove straight to Dan Myers's office. Dan's assistant announced him to her boss. The CEO's office was lined floor to ceiling with bookshelves surrounding an amazing ancient fireplace. Dan himself sat behind an old-fashioned executive desk that had belonged to the company founder, Russ Beckley. His blue eyes pierced Kevin's as he looked over the silver rims of his glasses.

"Thanks for seeing me, Dan," Kevin said. "I think there's hope for Alex."

Dan's eyebrows raised and he folded his arms, leaning back in his chair. "You really think so?" Dan asked.

"I believe so. I just left Alex talking with Quinn. Give him a second chance, Dan. He can change."

Dan polished his glasses. "I'll think about it, Kevin. But if working with Quinn doesn't help him, I don't think anyone could do better. For now, I'll believe with you . . . " Dan said, looking as if he were addressing someone not in the room.

2. Restart

When Quinn McDougall walked into Alex's hospital room, Alex was sitting propped up by pillows, blankly watching the monitor beside him. His right arm sported a blue cast. An exotic, octopus-like machine made by Beckley Medical was attached to his crushed left leg. A laptop was attached to the machine. *Prototype*, Quinn thought. "Alex Beckley?" Quinn said, taking Alex's good left hand and gently squeezing it. "I'm Quinn McDougall. How are you feeling?"

Alex studied his visitor. Quinn had wispy white hair and a ruddy face. A smile played at the corners of Quinn's mouth. He looked vaguely familiar.

"Better," Alex said. "The painkillers help."

Quinn settled into the chair next to Alex's bed. They talked about the accident and the hospital. Alex learned that when Quinn was young, he had also been confined to a bed, with both legs broken, for an entire summer—"My own close call," Quinn said. He confided to Alex that while he was laid up he had read incessantly, even memorizing favorite passages, and discovered he had an abnormally proficient memory. "I used it to get myself into Oxford and a good business school here in the States.

"My first career was at McKinley Partners just as it was becoming the top strategy consulting firm globally. I'm still on the board of McKinley, but now I am in a 'second half' role—as Bob Buford calls it in his book *Halftime*—as a consultant and advisor to a handful of executives and their companies.

"But what about you, Alex?"

"I've been thinking about your question, Quinn—about what I am going to do with this second chance."

"Go on."

"I need to change. I'm passionate about what I do. But I feel more and more uneasy, exhausted, and somehow isolated." Alex felt uncomposed and awkward under Quinn's steady gaze, but he pressed on. "I'm just not getting the results I want at work or at home. I'm getting the message from my family that so far I've been more than a little self-centered. It's been a lot about me."

"How's that been going?" Quinn asked.

"Not so good. Something has shifted with this accident. If I really do have a second chance, I'd like it to be less about me and more about my daughter, the company, employees, customers, and others. Still want to help me?" Alex looked up at Quinn, cringing a little.

Quinn had not diverted his eyes from Alex. Without hesitation, he said, "Oh yes, Alex, I do. I really do." Then he leaned back into his chair. "Say more. What do you really want me to know?"

"I'm struggling. Like I said, my company, my relationship with my daughter . . . " He closed his eyes and remembered Rachel disappearing through the hospital door. She hadn't been back. "My father passed away and we never quite understood each other. My daughter is angry. I thought I knew how to be a father and an executive. But what I have been trying just doesn't work. The harder I press, the worse our results have been. My dad started the company and I want to keep it going. But our performance has been getting worse, not better. Do you have any ideas?"

"Yes," Quinn said, leaning forward in his chair. "Can I tell you a story?"

"By all means."

"It begins at my old firm. I had been noticing that many of the great strategies that we helped our clients develop never really went anywhere. So on a hunch, I started analyzing our files, making a stack of the reports from client engagements where our strategy work was never fully implemented or ultimately failed to achieve results. Soon I had to move the pile from my desk to the floor because it was growing too tall. On my desk I kept the small stack of reports of client companies whose performance improved steadily."

Quinn stood up and paced the room. "I dug into the stacks," he said, pointing to two invisible stacks, and Alex saw the gulf between them. "The high-performance clients were remarkable. Performance and achievement were evident throughout. All these companies were *powerful combinations of high purpose and high performance*. I had to see how these companies did it. So I asked the firm for a sabbatical to study these companies. My partners granted the time—provided I would report back on what I learned. For just over a year, I carefully researched these organizations. Well, more than researched. You might say that in a way I joined them . . . joined their adventure to do good and do great."

"Adventure?" Alex asked.

"Yes." Quinn smiled. "And by this time, I had met your father."

"Was Beckley Industries one of the successful companies?" Alex asked.

"Not quite," Quinn said. "Not that it was a bad company; Beckley just hadn't been able to get to the next level. The company was good—still is good—just not yet great. Your dad, Russ, and I became friends, and I shared with him the findings from my study of high-purpose–high-performance organizations. It was a good time for him to hear about my findings. The company had plateaued. Your dad was ready to try something different."

Even through a drug-induced haze, Alex could tell that Quinn was suddenly struggling to maintain his composure.

"Your dad was a good man—and my friend. We never got to implement the full approach. When he got sick, he pushed his doctors for the most aggressive treatment, even though the odds were poor. He told me he hoped that you would come back to help. Russ had so much more that he wanted to do."

"I know," Alex said. "Truth be told, that's part of why I agreed to come back now. I wanted to grow the company from where he left off. But instead, I am apparently bringing it down. So if you really have a different way, I'm ready to hear it, Quinn."

"I'm ready to help you do more than hear it, Alex. I'm ready to help you learn and implement this approach at Beckley." While Quinn was talking, two nurses came into the room. They gently rolled Alex over onto his stomach. To Alex's surprise, Quinn got down on the floor to keep talking.

From this humbled position, Quinn continued, "In the high-purpose–high-performance files, I discovered *five key practices* for leading differently and implementing a strategy that creates an enduring competitive advantage. I found a way to depict them as the points of a star."

Quinn got up and pulled the paper placemat from Alex's food tray and laid it on the floor. On it, he drew a star.

"Alex, as you recover, I'd like to show you how to put the five practices to work in your organization and, really, in your life."

"I've probably taken the company backward with my top-down, 'take no prisoners' approach," Alex admitted reluctantly.

"From what I hear, that's true," Quinn agreed.

Alex was quiet for a moment, mildly taken aback by Quinn's agreement. He gathered himself and went on. "Dad was a classic entrepreneur and a hard charger. I had no idea that he was up to something new. We didn't have many conversations after I left for Boston." Alex cringed. "I guess I didn't stay in

touch so well. I regret that now, of course, being the prodigal
. . . " Alex paused and looked again at the star that Quinn had
drawn. It triggered something in his memory. "He also drew
a star once for me—told me he was learning about 'meaning
and purpose.' I didn't think much of it at the time. Quinn, I'm
still not sure why you would be willing to help."

Quinn replied, "This is my personal Greater Goal—what
I live for."

Alex looked away. "I don't know what I live for."

"Well, fortunately, that's where we start." Quinn picked up
the star again. "The first practice is about your Greater Goal."

3. The Greater Goal

Quinn wrote words next to the star and pushed the placemat toward Alex.

Commit to the Greater Goal

"The Greater Goal? Mine or the company's?" Alex asked.

"Both actually," Quinn responded.

"If you're talking about the Beckley mission and vision statements, we have those: I read them. They are pretty good."

"This is deeper, Alex. The Greater Goal describes the very best you aspire to for customers, employees, and frankly, the world. But it's more than a description. It should effectively call each person and team to give their absolute best. It provides the strategic frame for determining what business you should be in to add the most value. It's not just naming the mission and vision; it's the process of committing to them and acting together on them that makes the difference."

"I need a little more help with that," Alex said. "How is that different from our mission and vision?"

"Let me be clearer with some examples, if you would allow me. I have a client that is a world-class healthcare organization by today's standard. Its mission and vision are centered around 'delivering the best possible care' to every person who comes its way. When the leaders began to ask new questions about their true Greater Goal, it changed the entire organization—for the better."

Alex sat up a little straighter. "I would write this down if I could write," he said, looking at the hand cast.

"No worries," Quinn said with a smile. "I think I might just take you to see this organization for yourself. Wrestling with their Greater Goal was a watershed chapter for these leaders." With that, Quinn pulled a fresh three-by-five card and a beautiful fountain pen from his jacket pocket. "In the example I'm thinking of, the mission to provide healthcare services was important but was still not enough. The organization could do more. The leaders believed a Greater Goal would include keeping people healthy, promoting wellness, and preventing people from coming in for repair medicine in the first place."

Alex broke in, " . . . and they could make money at that?"

"You bet," Quinn said. "Their Greater Goal first led them to consider this larger aspiration and then led them to *reconsider their existing business model* and put in place a new model that served customers in a new way. They figured out how to make money offering total health care—preventative as well as repair medicine. They are reinventing themselves led by their Greater Goal. And just in time too. They are actually bending the cost of health care in the right direction by helping many people stay healthier."

Quinn sketched notes on the card for Alex. It said:

> • The Greater Goal goes beyond mission and vision to create a new identity—a greater strategic frame—allowing for new value propositions, new services, new customers, and a new business model of proactive health care.
>
> • This strategic approach reframes the entire workplace, energizes employees, and serves as an innovative example of health care that works for all.

Alex probed further. "How about some other examples?"

"Sure," said Quinn. "I know of a financial services firm that expanded on its mission of asset management. The firm crafted a Greater Goal to help families and foundations steward their wealth in highly effective ways based on personal values and goals. This led the firm to become more expert in spotting investments consistent with those clients' values. It managed risk with better statistical, financial, human, and ethical approaches. It even offered low-cost financial services to key nonprofits supported by its clients."

"It sounds like a formula to go out of business," Alex remarked.

"Far from it. This firm has become one of the most successful in its industry. Another example is a military organization that is putting resources into building schools and bridges. Its people are making friends in pursuit of the Greater Goal of peace.

"In another case, a biopharmaceutical organization went beyond focusing on its molecule pipeline to include the perspectives of the patient, payer, and provider all in an integrated approach to total disease management.

"And another favorite of mine is a city roads and traffic department that went from potholes to purpose. It adopted a Greater Goal of connecting families and businesses with roads that work. That led the department to enlist the public in spotting potholes when they were small and easily repairable—before they became a bigger problem. It discovered better repair materials and even enlisted local university brainpower to predict pavement breakdowns and simulate the best maintenance schedules and best alternative traffic flows around repairs. I have examples from almost every industry and sector."

"Give me one more," Alex said, smiling.

"Okay," Quinn responded, pointing just above Alex's head and then slowly bringing his finger down to point directly at Alex. "I see a medical products company headquartered right here in the city reaching for a new Greater Goal. This leads to higher value created for existing and new customers and by a senior team committed to a cause and to each other." Quinn said, "You will be able to fill in the details of this one for yourself, Alex, if you choose."

Alex returned the smile. "Thanks for the examples and the challenge. I can see a bit better now. Give me that definition of the Greater Goal again."

"Okay, Alex. A Greater Goal has three specific dimensions. First, the goal is great in the sense that it aims for a greater good—hugely positive outcomes for many. Second, it is great because it requires the combined and aligned best efforts of everyone in the whole company. And third, it calls each of us individually to greatness, to give our very best and to become part of something great ourselves.

> • Greater Good
>
> • Aligned Efforts
>
> • Individual Greatness

"The Greater Goal represents the 'North Star' by which an individual or organization can navigate through changes and challenges."

"That sounds like what I need myself—what we need," Alex acknowledged.

Quinn smiled in agreement. "Alex, will you take a homework assignment?"

Alex indicated his busted right hand. "As long as it doesn't involve writing."

Quinn chuckled. "Mostly thinking. I want you to reflect on your heart's desire. What do you want your life to count for?"

Even as he heard it, Alex realized he'd never really thought about this question. "What do I want my life to count for?"

"Exactly." Quinn glanced out the door. "We will start with you and then get to what this looks like for your work and for the company. A writer I respect, Joel Kurtzman, said in his book *Common Purpose*, 'When leaders pursue higher goals, the results have been almost magical.' I know the nurse is going to come in and chase me out of here soon. So when we get together next time, let's talk about both your own and your company's Greater Goals.

"Here is the test, Alex. Greater Goals will be other focused. Your Greater Goals will not be about you but will define you."

Almost on cue, a nurse dressed in bright flowered scrubs came in. "Time to leave," she said evenly, as if she saw distinguished-looking gentlemen sitting on the floor every day.

"I was just on my way out." Quinn rolled up off the floor but bent down once more to address Alex. "Get better, Alex. Many people are waiting to help you."

Alex closed his eyes, already beginning to work on his assignment. It was a big question. As the drug pulled him into sleep he dreamed of what life could be.

Out in the hallway, Quinn called Kevin.

Seeing the caller ID, Kevin answered eagerly, "How was he?"

"We are a go." There was a pause on the other end of the line.

"Do you think he realizes that this is a test?"

"Possibly," Quinn said. "But he sincerely wants to change, Kevin."

Alex woke up the next morning thinking about purpose. An employee was cleaning the room—"an environmental services associate," according to the nametag. Michael had impressed Alex every day of his stay. Here was an opportunity to learn.

"Michael, you really like what you do," Alex observed.

"I love it," Michael said.

"Some could say that what you do every day . . . "

Michael finished the awkward sentence for him: "Makes me the low man on the totem pole?"

Alex smiled sheepishly.

"Nope," Michael said. "I like people and I like my team. Our team helps people like you. What we do is important; we keep patients safe from infection and make this place look good. Actually *we are all caregivers here*, including me."

"Did somebody named Quinn tell you to say that?" Alex asked jokingly.

"Who?"

"Just kidding. Thank you!"

That night Quinn called Alex's room to confirm Alex's commitment to working together, in case it was "the pain meds talking" when they last spoke.

"No, not the meds talking," Alex confirmed. "I want to hear more about this 'Star Model.' I'm up for working with you, Quinn."

"Good. Then how would you feel about my speaking with your team? I'd like to get their input on what is working and what is not."

"I'm afraid of what you will hear, Quinn."

"Fear not, Alex! Let's get it all out in the open."

Within two weeks, Alex was home again—but he had to use a wheelchair and sleep in the first-floor den. For the time being, he couldn't climb the stairs to the second floor, which he shared with Rachel and his mom. His company set up a special hospital bed in the den. His mom added her home-made quilts. That first night home he drifted off to sleep with plenty of medication on board. In semisleep he became aware that Rachel was sitting quietly in the room, just watching him. He wanted to speak to her, but he somehow couldn't.

The next morning he had another chance. Rachel was making a sandwich for herself in the kitchen. Alex wheeled in. "Rachel, I'm on a roll and I want to talk about me and you."

"Bad pun, Dad. I'm going to be late. Can we talk later?" But her attitude said *I don't want to talk at all.* "Sorry, I gotta go. I'm late."

Alex winced. *I've used those same words a thousand times.*

4. Healing

At noon on his first day home from the hospital, Alex heard his mother in friendly conversation on the front porch. A moment later she led Quinn through the front door by the arm. Alex realized instantly that if Quinn had once been his father's friend, then he was likely his mother's friend too. *But why have we never met before? Was I so distant from my parents' life that I did not know a close friend like this?*

"How are you?" Quinn asked as he strode into the den.

"Okay," Alex said. "I'm glad to be home. It's still a challenge with Rachel. I deserve it."

"Give it time," Quinn said. "Did you do your homework?"

"I did. It was hard."

Alex picked up the notepad and tossed it to Quinn. He had scribed awkwardly with his left hand since his natural writing hand was covered in a cast. "I started with the personal, then the company."

Alex was suddenly struggling for composure. "Quinn, I want this to be a family, a real family, again."

Quinn followed Alex's gaze to a carefully arranged group of photos within sight of the bed. They were pieces of a family, each in its separate frame. Alex had pushed them together.

Alex's note said simply, "I would love us to be a closer family."

"What more, Alex?" Quinn gently prodded.

"I want to help build a company that makes a difference," Alex said.

"What does that look like?" Quinn asked.

"We help people who are hurting. We help restore people to health. I want to invite everyone in the company to sign up for this."

Quinn let the comment hang in the air between them, allowing Alex to absorb what he had just declared. Finally, he said, "That's great, Alex. How often do you say that to people in the company?"

"I said something like that from the stage at my first annual meeting. These days I feel the need to talk more about shareholder value and earnings growth. Don't get me wrong—we wouldn't have a company without that."

"I believe you," Quinn said. "But as I said, the best organizations have both purpose *and* performance. Tell me if this captures what you just said." He pulled out his fabulous fountain pen, flipped to a new page in Alex's notepad, and wrote:

> Care for those who are hurting.
>
> Bring life and health to customers.
>
> Call others to the cause.
>
> FROM THE DESK OF *Alex*

When Quinn pushed the pad of paper back, Alex felt something stir in his chest.

"That's it, Quinn. That makes me happy."

"One of my favorite authors, Thomas Merton, who wrote *No Man Is an Island*, made this comment on giving: 'True happiness is found in unselfish love, a love which increases in proportion as it is shared.'" Quinn looked up. "I say, 'When you give, you get even more.'"

Alex's mom came in the room.

"I thought you both might like some tea," she said.

"Annie, you're wonderful," Quinn said, standing to help her. "Earl Grey! Thank you."

"It's good to have you here again, Quinn. Let me know if you boys need anything else."

"Thanks, Mom," Alex said. As she left the room, Alex turned to Quinn, holding his teacup gingerly. "She loves taking care of me and I love letting her.

"Quinn, I learned something from the hospital. All the people there identify themselves as caregivers. Not just the medical staff but the housekeepers, the transporters, the lab techs, and even the valet car parkers. It was powerful. They all seemed to relate personally to the mission of the place. They all called themselves 'caregivers.' We are also part of that at Beckley—I mean, we are all caregivers. I'd like that as part of our Greater Goal."

Quinn sketched. "This is you, Alex."

"You named your Greater Goal. Now imagine the power of a company of individuals, each heart aligned to a common Greater Goal." Quinn sketched again.

"Remember my 'two stack' analysis?" he said. "The highest-achieving companies focused on their higher purpose and also got higher performance. *The key was alignment to the Greater Goal.* Alignment to the purpose actually enabled high performance," Quinn continued. "Some of the lower-performing organizations had built purpose statements but failed to actually align everyone to a Greater Goal. Some other companies had performance cultures but failed to deeply engage the hearts of employees, so they ran themselves off the rails ethically or in other creative ways. Living by great values is part of the Greater Goal. It all wraps up into purpose."

Quinn pulled an edition of *Harvard Business Review* out of his battered briefcase. "Gary Hamel got it right in his article titled 'Moonshots for Management.' This is about the future of organizations—Management 2.0. He wrote that one of the great challenges facing management today is to *'ensure that the work of management serves a higher purpose.'*"

"So what do we actually do?"

"Let me tell you how one organization did it," Quinn said. "In fact, I'd say you're ready for a field trip. Let's go visit my favorite business school here in town. As an organization, they did it right."

"Really . . . a B-school. Wait, you mean my B-school? No way! I want to see this."

Quinn went to the front door to wait. Alex went to his closet and struggled to get a dress shirt on, and then he sat staring at his shoes wondering how to get them tied. While he was trying, Rachel came down the stairs. She didn't hesitate. Rachel knelt down and finished the job for her dad.

"Thank you, Rachel."

"I like to help you, Daddy."

"I'm going out for a while, Rach."

"Be careful, Daddy. Promise me . . . I can't lose you."

Promise me? "I promise, my daughter."

5. Benchmark

Quinn made a call to his friend the dean of the Kepper Business School. Doug Holiday was waiting for them at the main entrance of the school. This was Alex's old stomping grounds—back when he could stomp.

"Welcome back, Alex. Call me 'Doc'; everyone does. Come into the office." He led them to a room where an ancient desk complemented the modern space. Alex admired it.

Doc said, "It belonged to Thomas Mellon, who started a bank here in town. I keep looking through the drawers," he said, demonstrating by pulling out a hidden cubbyhole drawer, "looking for old stock certificates."

Quinn grinned and pointed out to Alex a framed star on Doc's wall.

Doc looked up at the star too. "Quinn claims we have done a decent job of gaining commitment to a Greater Goal—"

Quinn interrupted, "In spite of knowing every theory of strategy, change management, and leadership ever devised."

Quinn opened his notebook and sketched the star again. "As I said on the phone, we're here to look at the first practice of the Star Model. Alex is on a venture through all five practices." Quinn wrote "Commit to the Greater Goal" at the top of the star. "Alex wants to know how you set and gain shared commitment to the school's Greater Goal."

Commit to the Greater Goal

Doc stood and looked at Alex. "I envy you—learning this model for the first time."

Doc moved to sit on the edge of his massive desk. "Our 'company,' a business school, is a strange animal. It's a real business for sure, but it's one that has lots of mini businesses and many divergent goals. Singular alignment is a challenge."

Alex spotted another object over Doc's head. It was a framed business journal article cover.

> **BUSINESS REVIEW QUARTERLY**
>
> ---
>
> ### The Unlikely Transformation
> *of an*
> ### American Business School
>
> *Douglas Holiday, Ph.D.*
>
> ---

The frame also held a picture of a visibly happy team.

"Well, you must have made some progress," remarked Alex, pointing out the article.

"We did, all of us together. Here's how we ended the article." He flipped open a reprint of the article and showed Alex the last sentence: "An organization aligned, individual by individual and team by team, to a shared Greater Goal is one of the most powerful forces for good on earth."

"I believe you. But how did you gain buy-in to a shared Greater Goal?"

"We began by asking everyone, and I mean literally everyone who worked here, what he or she saw as the Greater Goal for the school. At the entrance to the school we placed a bulletin board inviting anyone and everyone to put their thoughts about the school's Greater Goal on index cards.

"That started something. Hundreds of cards were created. Then, this being a tech-savvy school campus, a group of students built an online board with virtual cards.

"The online version took off. Alumni, administrators, faculty, students, and even prospective students got involved."

Quinn joined in. "It went viral. Our stakeholders experienced the magnetic pull made possible when everyone is genuinely engaged."

Doc continued, "We asked, 'What do you really aspire to be? What does the world need from us? What do we value? What is good for the corporations where our students will ultimately work? How do we focus on doing good, along with doing well?'"

Doc opened a drawer in the antique desk and sifted through a few papers. "Finally, the time came when we needed to meet physically to align to a Greater Goal for the school. I sent invitations out."

Invitation from Doc Holiday
Please join us for a Greater Goal Experience
September 7 at the Campus Field House
Together we will dream about what our
school can become.
We will aim high, craft a shared "Greater Goal,"
and begin the process of aligning and
committing to our goal.
With hope,
Doc
RSVP to the dean's office
PS We really need YOU!

"And guess what?" Doc asked.

"What?" Alex said automatically.

"Everyone came!"

"Everyone?" Alex asked, astonished.

"Yep! We had to move to a bigger place. We moved the group to the biggest warehouse we could find on campus. Quinn and some of his wizard helpers facilitated us. We wrote on movable whiteboard walls to gather and synthesize ideas. We debated, deliberated, and decided—and we all owned it! In the same day we aligned to a Greater Goal, crafted strategic rules on how to get there, and even agreed on some key team-based initiatives. An amazing day."

"And what was your shared Greater Goal?" Alex asked.

"As Quinn would say, the first thing about our Greater Goal is that it's not about us. It's about our students. The Greater Goal statement we crafted was: *We Are Leaders Serving Leaders. Together We Will Learn, Teach, and Serve.*'"

Quinn interrupted. "And the shared commitment sparked a real transformation."

Doc looked at Alex, "Oh, and by the way, bad news, Alex. I checked and you are still one class short of graduation." Alex's jaw dropped. Doc smiled broadly, "Just kidding. I hope this helps you guys."

"Thanks, Doc," Quinn said. "That was great. I need to get the patient home."

Quinn drove Alex back toward Point Breeze in the East End of Pittsburgh. Alex was still reeling. "Who would have thought this could happen in my old B-school . . . When I was there, it was more like 'faculty first.' To hear the faculty embrace a 'student first' approach is amazing. I see what they did. What else would you say about the first practice, 'Commit to the Greater Goal,' Quinn?"

"A couple of things, Alex. Underneath the practice are a couple of key principles for you to consider as you think about implementation at Beckley."

Quinn shifted in his seat to reach into his back pocket. "I hoped you would ask, so I have another card for you, Alex. I'm old school, so you'll get these handwritten." He handed Alex the slightly bent card.

Practice One: Commit to the Greater Goal

Principles:

- Your Greater Goal is not about you.

- The power comes from full alignment to the Greater Goal.

Alex was puzzled. *My Greater Goal is not about me?* He sat in silence, wondering what that meant.

6. Feedback

Driving back from the visit to Kepper, Quinn turned onto Thomas Boulevard and parked in front of the Beckley home, a classic American foursquare craftsman house. One could imagine it new in the late 1800s, projecting confidence in the future.

Alex asked, "What are you hearing from my team in your interviews?"

"Do you want to go through this now, Alex? It's been a big day for you already."

"I want to hear it—the good, the bad, and the ugly."

"Well, then, why don't we go inside? My friend Ken Blanchard calls feedback 'the breakfast of champions.' I have my notes with me. If you will make the tea, I will provide the feedback." The two men went inside, chatted of this and that while making their tea, and then sat down together.

"I'm ready," Alex said, but his body said, "I'm nervous."

Quinn began. "It is clear to everyone that you bring energy and drive to Beckley. But the practices you brought to the company carried unintended consequences."

"Ouch, that sounds bad." Alex winced.

"Your intentions were good—everyone recognizes that." Quinn reached in his briefcase and pulled out a folder. "I interviewed all the members of your senior team to get their very best thinking on several key purpose and performance questions, and I learned that they have common perceptions about what's working and what isn't. Naturally, I also got some outlier responses, and those can be very helpful. But first let's look at the strengths that were described, then we'll look at what's not working.

"Strengths included a near-unanimous value for hard work, a tradition of customer service, a culture of innovation, a desire to grow, and a willingness to change. Your team members believe in the values upon which the company was founded and feel a strong sense of calling to a higher purpose that the business can fulfill." Quinn looked over his reading glasses at Alex. "But there has been some erosion of the focus on values and purpose lately."

Alex flinched a little but invited Quinn to go on. "Tell me more about what isn't working."

"Okay, here are my notes." Quinn handed Alex a report with the feedback organized under the following headings: Goal Setting, Collaboration and Internal Competition, Learning from Results, Customer Focus, and Financial Focus. Quinn navigated through the report, underlining key points as he went, and together they read and discussed each topic.

"First, I asked how the company currently set goals and learned that specific measurable goals are set for individuals throughout the company. Your good intention was to focus individual efforts and raise performance throughout the organization. However, too many goals, some contradictory to each other, led to confusion and discouragement.

"My recommendation to you is to put in place fewer, more focused and mutually shared goals, organized under one Greater Goal. Be equally clear about the values Beckley holds. Do good and do well."

Quinn added, "Establishing the Greater Goal will help here.

"Competition," Quinn said as he tapped on the next sheet with his pen. "You introduced *internal competition* between teams and divisions. You intended to create a climate of friendly competition. However, lots of *un*friendly competition emerged. You have the beginning of a win-lose culture." Quinn looked over his glasses again. Alex was getting familiar with that look. "And this may sting a little, Alex. Some on your team said it seemed to be about *your* winning, *your* succeeding, perhaps at the expense of others."

Alex sat back in his chair. He contemplated the ceiling awhile before he answered. "You're right, Quinn. That does sting. It hurts because it has some truth to it. I see now that it's not about my winning. It's not even about me at all. It's about helping everyone here succeed. Let me start there. What else can I do?"

Quinn tapped the paper again. "Here's the next recommendation: put in place interlocking shared goals. This will lead to collaboration instead of competition and to a win-win culture. Hold yourself and other leaders to the standard of serving others, not being 'self-serving.'"

Quinn went on. "Next finding. Your frequent after-action project and performance reviews focused mostly on the negative, on shortfalls and gaps. After-action reviews are generally a very good idea, Alex. But the unintended effect from overfocusing on the deficits has led to less risk taking and initiative in the company. I'd recommend that you focus specifically on identifying successes. Celebrate successes and try to understand why they happened; then build on those successes.

"And here is the last key finding, Alex," Quinn said. "Bottom-line profitability is paramount, overriding all other consider-ations. Your team pointed out, I would say 'admitted,' that the singular pursuit of profitability undermines long-term strate-gic thinking and results in cutting corners and may even lead to managing the numbers over telling the truth." Quinn had that look again over his glasses. "Dangerous stuff. My recom-mendation is to focus on building a healthy, growing, endur-ing company under the banner of a longer-term Greater Goal. Reconfirm your values. A strategy that is based on values and aligned to a Greater Goal will yield long-term sustainable profits."

Alex absorbed the words. "Ouch, this is painful. But frankly, this helps a lot, Quinn. How do we get back on track?"

"We are already on that journey. You will find that these 'new practices,' and a whole lot more, are embedded in the Star Model. Your team is ready. In fact all of this was pro-posed by them in the interviews. What does that tell you?"

"That I have a better team than I deserve," Alex observed.

The men talked for another hour before Quinn said good-bye. On his way home, Quinn called Kevin. "I would say that he passed a key test today. He owned the feedback and is ready to go."

As Alex prepared to go to sleep in his makeshift bedroom, he picked up the picture of Rachel. No matter what, tomorrow night he would hobble up the stairs and say good night.

But tonight, he would pack Rachel's lunch. He placed a note inside the bag and left the lunch on the kitchen table.

Rachel,

How about another chance?

I love you,

Dad

Alex had no idea how Rachel would respond to his request. It mattered a lot to him, but he was willing to wait for an answer and to keep trying to connect.

Tomorrow Alex was returning to his office at Beckley Medical for the first time since the accident. He felt a mix of emotions: fear, gratitude—a fresh start.

Sleep did not come easily.

7. Shared Goals

Beckley Medical was headquartered in a classic indus-trial building buried in the quiet heart of a Pittsburgh neigh-borhood. Inside the crisp, white-and-blue lobby, dozens of Beckley's products were proudly housed in display cases. A portrait of Russ Beckley, the founder, graced the room. Beyond the desks of the office administrators, Kevin Jordan and Quinn McDougall sat at a steel boardroom table.

"Alex has shown me something," Quinn was saying.

"I can see it too," said Kevin. "But the senior team is afraid he's going to come back and go right into his old ways. Alex handed out more goals than we can possibly meet. Then it was 'push and tell' or sometimes 'stop and yell.' I remember a football coach like that." Both men laughed at the image.

Quinn said, "Alex has made a good start on his view of the Greater Goal."

"Same here with the senior management team," Kevin added.

"So I suggest it's time to bring Alex and his team together," continued Quinn, "to finish drafting the Greater Goal as they see it. Then we can move on to the next key practice, 'Construct Shared Goals.'"

Kevin glanced out the window and saw Alex wheeling into the lobby. "Here he comes. At least he's not rolling and texting at the same time."

Alex Beckley rolled past the product displays in the lobby and straight into the conference room just as the senior team began arriving. He clasped hands with most of the team. A couple of people tried to awkwardly hug him as he sat in his high-tech Beckley wheelchair. Kevin called the meeting to order while Quinn drew the now-familiar star on the whiteboard at the front of the room.

Quinn said, "Alex, your team knows that you have been learning about the five actions of high-purpose–high-performance organizations." He tapped the large hand-drawn star on the flip chart and added the second practice.

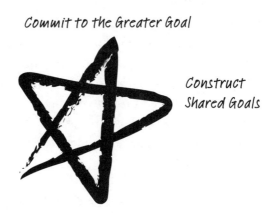

Commit to the Greater Goal

Construct
Shared Goals

"And in other news," Kevin said in the mock tone of a news-caster, "your team has been learning about the Star Model as well. We might even be a bit ahead of you in the learning curve. We hope that's good with you."

"More than good, that's great. Really great," said Alex. "It's amazing how much progress can occur when I'm not around." He saw nervous smiles all around the table.

Kevin spoke directly to Alex. "And we would love you to join us—to lead us."

Alex paused before he responded. "I wouldn't wish this on anyone, but my accident was a wake-up call and the down-time has given me an opportunity to reflect. I saw how I was living my life and leading this company. Not so good. Second chance?"

Uncomfortable glances were exchanged among the team.

"You bet," Kevin Jordan said. Others nodded their accep-tance.

Alex nodded his thanks and looked down at his leg cast. "I tried to drive . . . well, hard. Not such a good driver, I guess. All of you probably have a dozen or more goals apiece." He was surprised by knowing laughter from his team.

"Too many priorities lead to no priorities, I see that now. I believe we really need to start with one Greater Goal as our North Star and our greater purpose."

"One goal to rule them all," quipped Nate Strayer, the chief financial officer.

Quinn looked puzzled.

"What? You never saw *The Lord of the Rings*?"

Alex rolled his eyes to acknowledge the joke and then con-tinued. "So I now think it is crucial for this team, and then the whole organization, to deliberate about the Greater Goal for Beckley Medical."

"You must have some thoughts on it," Sally Smith, head of sales, prodded. "We have been going round and round in the team about what it should look like."

"Well, mine would only be *one* idea, not *the* idea," Alex said. "But I did have an insight while in the hospital. I think we need to talk about what we value, both individually and as a company. What is it that we care about so strongly that it gets us up and out the door each morning?

"By the way, I witnessed something powerful in the hospital that just might help us. What an engaged bunch! I mean everyone—from the doctors and nurses to the environmental services staff to the parking attendants and security guards. It was really amazing!"

"Tell them what you heard from Michael, the man on the housekeeping staff who spoke with you," said Quinn.

"Yes, Michael. His title was 'environmental services worker,' but he told me he saw himself as a caregiver—and an important part of the hospital team."

Alex let that sit with his team. Kevin again led the response: "We are caregivers here. We care for those who care for patients through our world-class products and services."

"Good, Kevin." Alex wrote "CAREGIVER" on the whiteboard. Alex looked over at Quinn for encouragement; Quinn winked. It was enough. Alex proceeded.

"Let's work on our Greater Goal," Alex said, tapping the whiteboard to indicate where he would write down their input. "Let's push ourselves beyond our stated mission and vision to build something together. We are looking for something that will be *hugely positive* for many—our customers and perhaps other types of customers we haven't even thought of yet."

Kevin added, "And something that will call for the *collective contribution* of all of us and call each of us *individually to greatness*. By the way, did I ever tell you all about the last championship year I had in pro football?"

Everyone groaned in mock agony while smiling in good humor. They had all heard many of Kevin's pro football stories. He was used to their groans and laughed good-naturedly.

"Moving on," Alex said, laughing. "Let's brainstorm around elements of our Greater Goal. You have all been working on your thoughts. I'll record," Alex volunteered. The ideas started coming from the engaged team quickly. They included

- It's a great idea to think of ourselves as caregivers alongside other caregivers.
- What if our Greater Goal included more than the hospital experience—the full range of health care?
- Let's aim to keep people healthy with products that monitor and promote health.
- Let's have products that follow patients home to continue their healing.
- What if we make our products radically more affordable, even by developing countries?
- What if we added "new to the world" types of innovations to our aim?

The senior team's brainstorming went on for a good while. At the end, Alex helped summarize. "I think what we've done is assemble the outline of our Greater Goal." He moved back and looked at the whiteboard. "It's like we are assembling the border pieces of a jigsaw puzzle. I recommend that we pull out pieces from our brainstorm that both most resonate with us and stretch us. Then let's take that outline to the rest of the company."

"The rest of the company?" Nate responded with alarm in his voice.

"Yes, the company, Nate." Alex turned back to the rest of the team. "What resonates with all of you and would stretch us?"

What emerged was this:

> Aim for the full continuum of care beyond the hospital setting.
>
> Create genuinely innovative products and services.
>
> Adopt the point of view of a caregiver. Become part of the team.
>
> Aim to enhance life and health with our products and services.
>
> Join the company to a cause—health and life.

"I agree," Alex said. "What do the rest of you think?"

Nods of approval showed clearly that the majority agreed.

"Okay, then," Alex continued. "Let's pull it together." Alex penned a draft Greater Goal on the board: "We aspire to create innovative products that enhance life and health worldwide. We are caregivers and life enhancers."

Nate said, "I expect it will be a messy process and take a lot to gain buy-in throughout the company."

Sally rebutted in a lovely West Virginian accent, "I think they are all hungry for this, Nate. They'll come on board."

Alex could see Quinn sketching something across the table. When Quinn was finished, Alex reached across the table and pulled it to him and smiled.

"I love it!" exclaimed the head of marketing, Angel Cabre. "This has all the elements of a strong brand, positioning, and purpose." Alex respected Angel's talent and was glad to see her energized.

The head of human resources, Matt Joachim, touched her arm. "Our associates want this connection to our customers . . . I know I do."

"That's why I came here years ago," said Dr. Stan Ralston, the vice president of research and development, known to all as "Dr. Stan." Others joined in. "Me too." "Yes!" Agreement and alignment were happening.

Only Nate, Alex's friend from his days working in Boston, failed to join in. "Hey, I'm committed to taking care of the numbers for this organization," Nate said.

Alex considered his friend's comment. *Something is off.*

"Okay, we have drafted input for Beckley's Greater Goal. We will firm this up by involving the rest of the company."

"I've got something for us." Quinn pulled papers out of his briefcase and began passing them around. "Let's go on to the second practice, *'Construct Shared Goals.'* In my experience, this is the key to catalyzing aligned, collective action. You might say the point of the Star Model is *shared goal achievement.* Let's see what it would take to create interlocking shared goals among this team."

Quinn looked over his reading glasses. "Many organizations have learned that traditional goal-setting approaches can make performance worse. They can unintentionally create internal competition, short-term thinking, and poorly coordinated work across departments. But creating *shared* goals, where we commit to collective success, commit to each other, and align to the Greater Goal, can really work."

"Are we just going to *hear* about this stuff or *do* it?" Tony Falcon, the operations vice president, asked.

"Yeah, Tony," Alex encouraged.

"Do it," Quinn said. "We have a draft Greater Goal. Now, how would this team go about constructing shared goals that could move the company toward that Greater Goal?"

John Wilson, the strategy vice president, spoke up: "I guess we'll have to agree on the critical success factors that must be in place—factors like being the provider of choice. It becomes a strategic goal to make these critical success factors a real competitive advantage for us. We will need to analyze business processes that underlie those factors. Our key business processes must be excellent to distinguish us. Then we design the initiatives or projects to improve our business processes. It's all about strategy design and execution."

"Exactly," Quinn encouraged. "Each strategy is *how* you will achieve the Greater Goal. Each *what* you agree on per strategy is a shared goal." Quinn quickly sketched on the whiteboard.

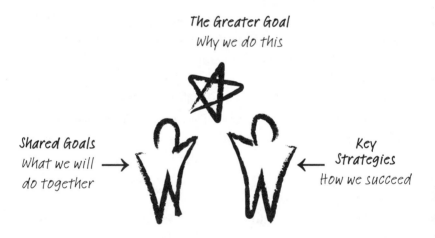

"This is the why, the what, and the how together," Quinn said.

By the end of the morning, colorful scribblings of shared goals and strategies—whats and hows—covered the

whiteboard of the conference room. The team whittled the
profusion of ideas down to the five top company strategies
and five top shared goals. Shared goals were to be equally
owned by each member of the senior team. Privately, Quinn
commented to Alex, "Shared goals call for *shared leadership*,
Alex. We'll talk more about that later."

Over lunch, the team's conversation launched into how
they could validate and create buy-in to the Greater Goal,
strategies, and shared goals throughout the company. Dr.
Stan offered his usual sage counsel. Nate spoke only when
spoken to.

Quinn was drawn into advisor mode. He offered, "Get an
empty warehouse. You can divide up the space with movable
whiteboard walls and screens. The local B-school did this and
created a similar event. We can use group ideation methods
to facilitate input."

Together, the senior team designed a two-day off-site. The
first day would be spent confirming the Greater Goal individually and collectively, making the meaning together. This
would be an opportunity for the senior team to both listen
and lead. The second day would be spent cascading the company strategies and shared goals into and across departments.
Quinn acted as their guide to plan how each executive would
facilitate the process.

By the end of the day, the team sat in front of a list of guiding principles for the off-site workshop that would aim to get
everyone involved and offering his or her best thinking. A
road map for the two days came next, headed up with one of
Quinn's doodles, followed by a bulleted list of the workshop's
objectives.

Align to the
Greater Goal!

- Before the off-site, communicate the purpose of the days
  and give directions for prework. Ask people to think about
  personal and company values, our shared purpose, and
  possible strategic breakthroughs.

- During day one, create a vivid composite picture of who
  we are as a firm—our identity and history. Look together
  at the underlying values we are living out. Ask everyone to
  participate in describing our desired future and what kind
  of community we could be together. Note any differences
  in the values we aspire to.

- By the end of the first day, summarize the mutual
  understanding of Beckley Medical's Greater Goal.
  Determine what level of commitment has been achieved.

- On day two, create shared goals in support of our Greater
  Goal. Intentionally bring together departments and teams
  that must work together to achieve shared goals, even
  those currently in conflict.

- Aim for company-wide alignment to the Greater Goal,
  commitment to Shared Goals and Strategies, and mutual
  support for each other.

What is success? Genuine alignment to the Greater Goal.

The executives sat back for a moment, each in thought. The possibilities offered by the off-site were growing, as was the sense that this could be big for the company. Some people felt uncomfortable with the scope of the work alignment of the whole organization to the Greater Goal. This was a major undertaking. Most sensed a growing awareness that, while leading this change was a big aspiration, this team was in it together and together it was possible. Each senior team member committed to a role in planning and facilitating the off-site.

Various practical matters were then addressed: "Where can we bring our whole company together?" "How will we deal with our entire staff being away from their jobs?"

"Being away for two days will require some serious coordination," said Alex. "We'll have to think that through together, but I have a few thoughts. It will certainly take some planning and notification that we'll be away. We could hire temporary help to monitor and communicate with us regarding emergent issues. Let's each bring issues and options to our next planning session. As far as where to hold the off-site, Quinn has a suggestion."

Quinn described a warehouse space in Pittsburgh's East Liberty neighborhood, where the two-day event could be held. Once a grand old city neighborhood, the East Liberty community had struggled with poverty, despite being on the edge of a vibrant and growing region of "meds and eds"— enormous investment in medical and technology research universities. But over the past decade, East Liberty constituents had banded together with a new Greater Goal—a community that works for everyone. And it was working.

After a spirited digression into community building, the group adjourned the planning session. Quinn and Alex met alone in the Beckley lunchroom and debriefed the senior-team meeting.

"Alex, tell me what you are seeing."

"Is this a coaching thing, Quinn?" Alex gave him a sly smile.

Quinn encouraged him. "Good leaders get better by continuously observing, reflecting, learning, changing, and . . . well, growing."

"I'm usually going too fast to reflect, so this will require using some dormant muscles," Alex began.

"What is clearer to you now?" Quinn asked.

"The Star Model, even though you are unveiling only it one practice at a time."

"Patience," Quinn said. "One day at a time."

"I get the Greater Goal as the North Star. I see what it just did for my team. I am excited to use the same process throughout the whole company. And I really like *shared goals*. Having fewer but crucial shared goals arranged around our key strategies is *way* better than my approach of giving everyone multiple, individual goals to achieve. I can see how I was suboptimizing our efforts."

Quinn stood up. "On that note, do you mind if I tell you another story? This one is personal. When we first met I told you about my accident, where I managed to break both legs."

"Yes, what happened?" Alex prodded.

"It doesn't make me look too smart. When I was a young man, back when the earth was still cooling, I was adventurous. I was traveling the Continent—that's Europe, you know—on a rock-climbing adventure on Mallorca with some friends. We started out hooked together, but I wanted to make it to the summit first. Like you, I can be more than a little competitive. I unhooked and climbed alone. It went well, until, well, it didn't. I fell about forty feet—a near fatal fall. It broke my legs and my pride. My team got me home alive. Having shared goals is like roping in and climbing together as a team."

Quinn went silent to give Alex a chance to reflect.

"Something tells me you have another card for me on shared goals, don't you?" said Alex.

Quinn slyly drew a three-by-five card from his jacket pocket and handed it to Alex.

Practice Two: Construct Shared Goals

Principles:

• *Real teamwork is enabled by shared goals.*

• *Shared goal achievement is in turn enabled by shared leadership.*

"Love it," Alex said.

Just then, his assistant stepped in. "Nate Strayer asked me to set up a meeting with you. And your daughter called while you were in session with your team."

"Her message?" Alex asked.

"She just called to see if you were okay. Sweet girl. You are okay, aren't you? I said you were."

Quinn looked at Alex over his reading glasses. "She's just worried. She almost lost her dad. Find a way to hang out with her. Do something you both will enjoy. Create a shared experience."

Alex laughed. "Thanks for sharing, Quinn. I will."

8. Unintended Consequences

A week later Alex got a very early morning visit from Matt Joachim, the head of human resources.

"Have a seat," Alex said, waving him in. The two men caught up on a few personal matters before they got down to business.

"What's up, Matt?" Alex finally prodded.

"Well, since our team meeting last week, I've been thinking a lot about alignment and doing some investigation on my own."

"Great!" Alex encouraged.

"This has been right under my nose, but I'll just tell it to you straight up. I've been wondering why we have so many medical products in the pipeline barely inching their way forward. What could be going on here? I'm no engineer, but I am a pretty good human resources guy."

"You are," Alex agreed.

"Well, I started interviewing our engineers, asking what they were doing day to day—how they were spending their time and allocating their efforts to products—and I found something rather remarkable and disturbing."

"You have my attention," Alex noted and he leaned forward.

"Each engineer," Matt continued, pushing a graph across the table to Alex, "has been distributing time across an average of six or more products."

Alex studied the graph and said, "I see," when, in fact, he didn't.

"Let me explain," Matt went on. "In effect, the engineers were distributing themselves across multiple products because they weren't sure what the real priorities were and in case any one of these projects failed, they'd still have job security. That's our fault." He looked up at Alex. "Our fault, meaning us—the senior management team. We weren't aligned enough to make big bets on high-priority, breakthrough projects and then help them succeed."

Alex understood and was stunned. "What next?" he said as much to himself as to Matt.

"I think we're all ready to stop what's not working—the projects that everyone knows don't really have a chance of succeeding. Let's align as a senior team and then align our best talent with our best breakthrough opportunities. We need to assure our engineering and scientific talent that if these newly focused, higher-priority opportunities do not succeed, they still have jobs."

"Let's get to work," Alex said, "changing our project-prioritization process."

"And," said Matt, "our talent management approach."

"Agreed. Let's work together on this, Matt."

9. Challenge

The next day, Alex wheeled down to Nate's office. Once the two friends were in conversation, Alex quickly realized that Nate was more than a little upset.

Nate politely inquired about Alex's health, his daughter, and his mother and then launched into his grievances. They were mostly directed at Kevin, Quinn, and the "Greater Goal thing."

"I can't believe you're supporting this stuff," Nate said, practically sneering. "What happened to you? Did the crash rattle your brain?"

Alex just listened. He had brought Nate into Beckley with him. When Nate finished, Alex said, "Nate, give this a chance. I need you."

Nate frowned and twisted in his chair. He wasn't happy, but he agreed, "Okay, you've got me, boss." But as soon as Alex left, Nate called several other people in the company to commiserate and conspire to resist the "Greater Goal Takeover." He had to save the company and save Alex from himself.

Quinn drove Alex home that night. Alex was quiet, but Quinn drew him out. "Quinn, I like what we're planning with this warehouse session, but it is different from anything I've ever done. What if people don't participate or buy in?"

"Like Sally said, I think the company is hungry for this. Still, why don't you 'roll the halls' and ask for support?"

"Ask for support?"

"You bet. And I expect you will get it."

Alex sat in the den that night, fiddling with spreadsheets. He was so lost in thought that he didn't hear or see Rachel slip into the room. She announced herself.

"Ah, hey Dad. Thanks for putting that note in my lunch. Mom used to do that," Rachel said and stepped forward. "It surprised me. I've been thinking a lot about our family. I want to try again."

Alex held out his arms for a hug. "Thank you, Rachel. Let's hang out together sometime, do something we would both enjoy."

"I've actually been thinking the same thing, Daddy," Rachel responded. She plopped down in Alex's leather chair. "Mom started teaching me about cooking, but then she got sick. We never really got back to it."

"Your mom was some cook." Alex fell quiet, remembering his wife buzzing around the kitchen.

"I know, Dad. And you're a really *terrible* cook." She was looking at Alex with an impish grin. "I would still love to learn how to cook, and you could really use the help. Grandma always does the cooking here, but if we got good at it, we could help her out. We could learn together. What do you think?"

The old Alex would have found a way out of this, but the new Alex said, "How do we start, Rachel?"

"Why don't we make a plan, like you always do for work? We could use your flip thing," Rachel said, pointing to the flip chart in Alex's office-bedroom. "I can write for us." And in her careful printing, Rachel scrawled the outline of a plan for Alex and daughter to cook together.

- Pick a meal that sounds delicious.

- Look for instructions on the Internet.

- Ask Grandma to be our coach.

- Shop for the ingredients at the co-op market.

- Have a feast every Saturday night!

The next day could not come quickly enough for Alex. He; his mother, Annie; and Rachel were up early and in the car quickly, with Mom at the wheel. Alex felt unsteady on his new crutches, and the prospect of grocery shopping with the girls had him feeling completely awkward. Rachel studied his tense face.

"Don't worry. It'll be okay. It's just grocery shopping. Other dads do this and live."

Upon entering the co-op market, Rachel took charge and disengaged a shopping cart from the line. "Do you have the list, Dad?"

"Yep, right here." Bracing himself on one crutch, he handed off a crumpled list.

The differences in father and daughter became clear right away. Alex wanted to go strictly by the list, checking off one item at a time. Rachel, on the other hand, wanted to be a bit more experimental. She was like her mother. On the spot she thought up interesting alternate ingredients and insisted on buying spices that Alex had never even heard of. But despite their differences, they were talking and they were laughing. They were working together.

At the checkout counter Rachel shared the whole cooking story with the cashier.

"Gee . . . I wish I could do that with my dad," the young cashier said.

"You can," Rachel encouraged. "If we can do it," she looked over at Alex with a wink, "you can too."

As they were leaving the co-op, a disheveled man approached and asked Alex for spare change to get some food. Alex hesitated, shielded Rachel, and looked down at the sidewalk. But Rachel stepped around Alex and offered her hand. She looked the man in the eye. "Hi, I'm Rachel. Did you say you're hungry? What's your name?"

"What? My name . . . my name is John . . . John J. Williams," the man stammered.

"Glad to meet you, John. This is my dad, Alex. Dad, couldn't we ask Mr. Williams to join us for our 'feast' on Saturday?"

Alex was alarmed. "Well . . . ah . . . I guess . . . " He shot Rachel a look of shock, but it did not stop his daughter. On she went.

"Why don't you come? We live just a couple of blocks away at 6955 Thomas," pointing over toward their block. "Come on by. In fact, we are going to do this every Saturday, so come whenever you can. We're going to start cooking around five o'clock and, well, we're kind of new at this, so we might need some help if you want to eat before eight."

"Okay," John said. "Thank you."

Alex was happy to get away. "Rach, you can't go inviting strangers to the house. It's dangerous!"

"It's my home too, isn't it, Dad? And besides, he looked hungry and sad. In school we talk a lot about how to reach out to people in need, right in our path. I thought I could invite him because you'd be there to watch over me."

"I love your heart, Rachel. I just want you to be careful."

Silently Alex was proud of his daughter. Remembering the embarrassed looks exchanged with the homeless man, he was sure this was the last he would see of John J. Williams.

10. Join the Company; Join the Cause

On a bright Monday morning in a rented warehouse in East Liberty, Quinn, Alex, and the senior team prepared to greet their guests. More than two hundred people would be present, including all of Beckley's management members and many other key stakeholders, would be present. As the guests flowed in, they passed a table stocked with tea, coffee, juice, bagels, and fresh sliced fruit. Fuel in hand, they made their way to the auditorium-like section of the warehouse, where dozens of microphones and a circle of chairs had been arranged. On the other side of the warehouse, Quinn and a half dozen facilitators had set up a forest of tall, movable whiteboards, laptops, projectors, wireless keyboards, rolling chairs, and tables. Images from Beckley Medical's past successes were moving across the walls in time with high-tempo music.

When everyone was seated, Alex stood up from his wheelchair and grabbed a new pair of Beckley ultralight aluminum crutches. Quinn sat nearby holding a giant to-go cup with a tea-bag label hanging over the side. Kevin Jordan sat in the front row with an iPad that would control the multimedia.

Scattered throughout the audience, the senior team watched Alex with smiles—and some worry hiding just below the surface of their faces. What had they gotten themselves into? Alex could feel his heart pounding under his ribs. He took a deep breath and began.

"It's good to be here. Frankly, it's good to be anywhere!" Anxious laughter rippled through the room. "My accident was both a stop and a new start for me." As Alex talked, Quinn watched the crowd. Every eye was intent on the man hanging on the crutches.

"When I woke up in the hospital," Alex said as he slowly raised his arm, still in a Beckley blue cast, "I found Beckley medical products all around me—and some in me. I know for a fact, we make great stuff."

Applause and smiles came from the people in the crowd, Dan Myers, Beckley's CEO, among them.

"We're good," Alex went on, "and we make great products. We actually help restore people to life and health." The applause was louder this time. "In fact, I believe we are all caregivers here." With that, the phrase appeared in ten-foot letters on the wall.

"Woohoo!" shouted a big man in the back. He didn't need a microphone. Others joined him in long and loud applause.

Alex grinned and said something into the microphone, but it was lost.

When the noise subsided, Alex began again, "We are all caregivers—through our world-class products and services. We propose this as part of our Greater Goal.

"Many of you know my friend Quinn McDougall. He's here to introduce you to a process by which we're going to consider and confirm our Greater Goal today—together. Quinn?" Alex gave a nod to his copresenter and then hobbled back to his wheelchair.

Quinn stepped forward. "Thanks, Alex and all of you, for inviting this outsider in. The Greater Goal of Beckley Medical should describe the best you aspire to for customers, yourselves, and indeed, the world. It represents what you value and your values. *It should call each person and team in the organization to give their best in pursuit of purpose and performance.*"

He continued, "A goal is *great* when it is enduring and full of high purpose. It is *great* when it calls all of us to align and work together." Quinn swept his arms about widely. "Finally, it is *great* when it calls each of us individually to be great and to give our best in service of something bigger than ourselves. Your Greater Goal should represent the North Star by which the company can navigate through both good and challenging times. Now to go over today's agenda, I'm turning the floor over to Kevin Jordan."

While Kevin walked to the front, music surged and a video showed Kevin's pro football highlights. The last clip showed him acrobatically catching a football over defenders in the end zone in a famous shot. This was a die-hard football town, so the noisy cheer got even louder. Kevin asked for quiet and advanced the slide presentation.

He began, "This is the game plan. We will today consider and confirm a Greater Goal for the company. This will stretch us to think about *where our products and services are most needed, what work we can be world-class at, and reconsider what businesses we should be in to add the most value.* This may provoke us to reconsider our positioning and our strategies. Next, we will construct shared goals, linking all our departments and teams together in a common purpose. Then in the weeks to come, your teams and departments will create breakthrough initiatives to reach for our Greater Goal. But this is also personal." Kevin walked to the front of the stage. "As Quinn said, this is also about signing up for something that only all of us can accomplish together." Kevin clicked the remote, and up came a slide: "One of the most powerful forces on earth is an organization fully aligned, team by team and individual by individual, to achieve a shared Greater Goal."

Commit to the Greater Goal

Construct Shared Goals

Alex struggled to his feet, faced the crowd, and spoke the words on the slide from memory, with feeling. "This is an invitation to join our cause. Together we will be one of the most powerful forces on earth . . . for doing good and doing well. The choice to join is yours."

Someone whistled and cheers broke out in the warehouse again.

"Let me extend a special welcome to some of Beckley's strategic suppliers," Alex said. The applause continued. "Perhaps you have noticed that we have posted some remarkable pictures of patients, clinicians, and others using our products. You will also find letters of thanks from around the world. Enjoy these reminders of the great things Beckley's products are doing."

Kevin cut in, "By the way, every picture and letter is authorized and compliant—there are no HIPAA privacy violations here." The legal folks groaned and others chuckled.

"We'll be gathering around these walls to deliberate about the Greater Goal for Beckley," Alex continued. "Facilitators will be around to capture your comments in real time, and we will be using this input to modify the draft Greater Goal statement so that we can confirm it, individually and collectively."

Quinn took the lead again, "Tomorrow's work will be developing strategies, breakthrough initiatives, and shared goals in pursuit of the Greater Goal. Facilitators will guide you through the process. You will also take time—and this is crucial—to write your own personal Greater Goal mission statements. That's right, each of you is going to come up with a statement explaining what you want to do personally to achieve the company Greater Goal."

Alex noticed people look at each other with smiles and delight.

As Quinn continued, a few Beckley team members were lining up along the outside aisles with stacks of paper. "You knew this was coming. These handouts summarize the input you gave us into our strategies and shared goals. You'll also see data about customer needs, experiences with our products, and aspirations. And at your tables, you'll see charts that show what we see as our comparative advantages and where our opportunities lie. You all provided this data. Get familiar with what others are thinking, ask questions, get clarity. Now we are going to put this all to work."

Kevin, every bit the former pro football player, exclaimed, "It's game time! Check your notebooks to see what discussion groups you are in."

The rest of the day was a fast-break but organized progress. Teams formed, worked, unzipped, reformed, and worked further. They debated, deliberated, and disagreed. But then more agreeing and aligning to a Greater Goal slowly emerged. The new Greater Goal included the idea of proactively enhancing health. That would put the company into new businesses with new kinds of products and services, such as home health care, monitoring, and prevention.

Alex, Kevin, and the senior team were everywhere, listening, leading, and encouraging alignment. Amazingly, within the space of a day, hundreds of people aligned to a Greater Goal. Each person—including Alex and Dan—wrote his or her own personal commitment to the Greater Goal.

The Greater Goal for Beckley Medical that emerged at the end of the day was reflective of the initial draft. But now it was *their* Greater Goal. Every person had been given the chance to reflect and create a personal picture of what these words meant to him or her. The new collective version was projected on the screen.

We Are Caregivers and Life Enhancers for the World

Through Our Innovative Products and Services.

This Is Our Company and Our Cause.

Now the Greater Goal belonged to everyone.

When Alex arrived home that night, Rachel was on the porch swing waiting for him. She moved over on the swing to make room for her dad, patting the spot where she wanted him to sit. The two sat quietly swinging for a while, watching fireflies in the yard. Alex waited for Rachel to start the conversation.

"Daddy, would you tell me something about what you did all day today? What did you like about your day?"

"I will," Alex said, scooting over a little closer to her. "I really like the people I work with, and today we got the chance to plan our future together. Tomorrow we are going to make plans to do good and great things." He stopped with that.

Rachel looked over at him. "I like that. Tell me more tomorrow when you come home. I'll be right here."

11. Shared Leadership

The next day the warehouse buzzed with excitement and anticipation. People talked in animated clusters over breakfast. Alex limped around on his crutches, listening to their conversations. He sensed people's excitement—now he would ask for their commitment. All of this enthusiasm was about to go to work!

CEO Dan Meyers stepped up to the microphone. "Today we will set shared goals for the company. This means we all share in the leadership of the company. Speaking for myself, this will be the first time I have been part of an opportunity exactly like this. I know that you may have some reservations about what we will accomplish and what can truly change. I personally believe we have a great future together, one where everyone can give his or her best, and we can create benefits for ourselves, our customers, and really, everyone we touch. I invite you to suspend your judgments and join me. Focus on your strengths, our new possibilities, and how we can make a difference together."

Dan turned the attentive audience over to Kevin Jordan, who announced the agenda and process for the day. Beckley's senior leadership team acted as facilitators, helping guide people together into predesigned small teams within designated areas of the open warehouse space. Each team space included a circle of chairs and large, movable whiteboards that functioned doubly as writing space and as walls between the teams. While on the previous day people had been situated in cross-functional teams made up of those who didn't always get a chance to work together, today they were organized by function, with their usual teammates. Day one of the off-site had been a refreshing change, and now, rejoining with their normal work groups, they felt renewed energy gained from a sense of new purpose, possibility, and perspective.

But to keep the cross-fertilization going, teams were placed strategically next to other teams to allow for occasional cross-functional collaboration. In particular, Alex made sure that Marketing's circle of chairs was right beside Research and Development's.

Above the marketing team, fluorescent lights hummed. A dozen people sat on black folding chairs arranged in a circle. The task was to consider the Greater Goal, develop supporting strategies, and design shared goals that included partnership with other functions to achieve them. Angel Cabre called the rowdy team to order.

"We must be in marketing heaven," she began. "We have the whole company joining *us* in focusing on a great big, really cool, *marketable* Greater Goal." Her arms waved in circles as she spoke, gradually spreading wider until she nearly hit the teammate sitting next to her. Laughter rose to the rafters.

"This is our chance to shine." She paused as the lights above them flickered momentarily. "Alex challenged us to create shared goals with other departments. Frankly, we have a bad track record with them." Angel gestured to the circle of people on the other side of the whiteboard—Research and Development.

"But we are joined at the hip with them in a lot of ways," she admitted. "We are both tuned into the 'voice of the consumer,' at least we should be. We listen for how to market while R&D listens to know what to develop. We both need to listen and then work together. So maybe we start by setting our own goals and then craft some shared goals to discuss with Research and Development. Can we do that?"

"I am skeptical that we can get to a better place with R&D," Sean Mallory interposed. "Someone in R&D will have a great idea, the team will research it on their own and develop a product, and a ton of support and energy will grow around it. The problem is that there may not be a real market for it. But the company produces it anyway, and then—*ta-da!*—we have another struggling product."

"So what do we need to do differently, Sean?"

"We need a real partnership," Sean said. "And I guess I'm willing to try."

And so they did.

Meanwhile, the research and development team was having a similar discussion as they worked on their goals, occasionally shooting glances at the marketing team.

By the midmorning break, both teams had finished their work. When they returned from the break, they combined all the chairs into one circle. Quinn joined them for the combined session, asking them to sit so that each team had people in every other chair around the circle. Alex sat nearby on wheels.

Each team was ready with a goal list on a PowerPoint slide. The research and development team projected their list first, and R&D's leader, Dr. Stan Ralston, read each bullet aloud. Angel did the same for the marketing team's list. As each point materialized on the screen, Alex heard some mutterings of "oh" and "huh" and "cool" from around the circle. A number of items from both lists were practically identical, even if the words were a little different. The statements were phrased as critical success factors or guiding principles. Each represented an important goal requiring shared commitment. Examples included

- New products must be driven by the genuine verified needs of our customers.
- Our customers are also looking to us for exciting new technology solutions that they may not even know they need yet. We must lead.
- We want to involve opinion-leader customers who have a sense of where the marketplace is going, not where it has been.
- As we step outside our core competencies, we must look for partners who can join us.
- We must build on our familiar, existing product platforms that customers love but also introduce innovative, new technologies on top of those platforms.
- We need to reinforce our brand but also introduce new products.
- We want to work with our Beckley counterparts in a better way.

- We must care for our customers' customers—the clinical caregivers' patients and their families—by providing products and services that delight them.

Angel typed up a slide combining the goals of both departments while the teams watched her work projected on the wall.

"Observations?" Quinn asked, looking around the circle. Several mouths were open and eyebrows rose in mild astonishment.

"It seems like . . . " Sean began, "like we *agree* on what success really looks like. I can't believe that *they* developed that list," he said half in jest.

"Well, I can't believe *you* developed that list," someone said from Research and Development in a mock aggressive reply. "Ha! Were you spying on us?" Now laughter broke out.

"It does look like each team could have made up the other's list," Angel said. "How about that?"

"So let's start drafting shared goals," Quinn encouraged.

Quinn doodled in front of the team. "Here's to supporting our customers together."

Shared Goals and
Shared Leadership

The teams brainstormed about what customers valued and what actions they could take together. They drafted a list of shared goals and what requests and offers needed to be made between the departments. Each team member made individual commitments to the shared goals in writing.

Next, Alex rolled to the finance team at Nate's request. To his surprise, Nate opened the conversation by saying, "I hope our president will lead us through this morning's exercise."

Alex stared back at him quizzically. In the circle of chairs, no one moved.

Nate then said, "Just kidding," and started the meeting. The team relaxed, but Alex did not. Alex sat through the session with increasing concern. At lunch, Alex talked with Nate and Dan Myers together.

"Nate," Alex said, "I am getting the feeling that you don't want to be here today."

"I'm fine," he said.

Dan leaned in close. "Nate." He said the name softly. "This can be the beginning of a real change at Beckley. It's a chance for us to lead in a new direction. If you can't support the direction, you and Alex must have a harder conversation."

"Fair enough, Dan," Nate said curtly. "I hear you." With that he got up and walked away.

Alex turned to Dan, shaken.

"This could be good, Alex," Dan assured. "Have that talk with Nate—sooner rather than later."

After lunch, in amazingly short order, each and every department had created shared goals and even aligned key strategic initiatives with other departments and teams. Team members wrote individual action plans, which were, in turn, aligned to the Greater Goal. This was what Quinn called "shared leadership" in action!

The interlocking teams posted their proposed shared goals and initiatives on their movable whiteboards and briefed the entire assembly, answering questions and receiving advice. It was apparent from the presentations that relationships had been improved over the past two days. Further deliberations to solidify agreements regarding shared goals were conducted on the spot and decisions made with key stakeholders in the room. Shared goal "owners" voted to rank the importance, urgency, and impact of the proposed initiatives relative to achieving the Greater Goal. Initiatives that missed the mark in terms of reaching the Greater Goal, or that were in direct conflict with each other, were revised. The agreed-upon initiatives were ranked in order of impact for further action planning and resourcing.

Alex could hardly believe it. *Within two days, they had gone from affirming a Greater Goal for Beckley Medical to creating genuine shared goals in pursuit of the Greater Goal.* Quinn was right: this was a better way. Why did he not see this before? Maybe he had to see it to believe it—or believe it to see it.

At the end of the day, the original breakout teams reformed at each of the many workstations to formally "check out." Each member got a chance to share her or his personal insights from the day and any words of appreciation.

Following the checkout, Alex gave his closing remarks and thank-yous, intending to close the session. But oddly, very few people left the building. They all knew that something remarkable had just occurred. They wanted to preserve and enjoy the moment. They continued milling around, looking at the initiative wall charts, and talking to each other, filling the room with cheerful noise.

In the back, one man, a production supervisor who had been with the company for years, grabbed a microphone. "I just wanted to say that I was thinking about retiring this year. But you know what? Ten thousand horses couldn't drag me out of here."

Others followed his lead and grabbed microphones. Comments and unscripted testimonies went on and on. At one point Alex anxiously looked over at Quinn for direction. Quinn simply mouthed the words "Just let it go."

A full hour later, Alex succeeded in closing the session with a second round of thanks. He sought out Quinn in the thinning crowd.

"Oh my God" was all he could say to Quinn.

"You got that right," Quinn responded.

On the other side of the room, Dan and Kevin were watching. Kevin leaned over to Dan with a sincere smile on his face and said, "Dan, this could be the beginning of a brand-new day for the company and for Alex."

Dan thought about that for a minute and responded in a way that caught Kevin off guard. "Alex still has a long way to go. He recognizes what is needed. He has set the stage. The people in this company know *what* is important to achieve as a group. Now they need leaders who can show them *how*. Alex's past habits may yet come back to derail him. These new goals—shared goals—they must be nurtured with a coach's hand, not a controller's. Alex has to take the initiative to serve this company in a new way."

Alarmed, Kevin stepped back from Dan's side and turned toward a window. Staring out into the distant Pittsburgh cityscape, he wondered aloud to Dan, "Do I understand you correctly that you don't think he can do it?"

Dan replied, "That's not it." He pointed to the city skyline, which was partially obscured by the foggy day's clouds. "None of us can see the path ahead with perfect vision. Alex must be resolute in helping us find clarity each day to guide us by our new North Star. He must show me that he can become a coach for his team. Otherwise, our goals will have been more clearly defined, but we will never reach them."

With that, Dan turned from the window, leaving a troubled Kevin looking out toward the Steel Tower as the late afternoon sun burned the fog away. Perhaps this was a good sign.

12. Community

Within a week of the warehouse session, Alex had three encounters that let him know things would never be the same at Beckley Medical. The first was with Matt Joachim, who called very early in the morning while Alex planned and pondered at his desk.

"Could I catch you before the staff meeting, Alex? I see you are scheduled pretty tight today, and I've got something I think you will want to hear."

"Sure, come on over."

"I'm here already," Matt said, literally finishing his sentence as he walked into Alex's office and plopped down on the couch.

"What's the good word?" Alex prompted.

"The word is *community*," Matt replied with a quickness that surprised Alex.

"Okay, go on, Matt. What's the story behind the word?"

Matt framed an imaginary picture with his hands, like a movie director. "I've been seeing something odd in the lunchroom. I eat there every day, and I noticed there was, well, something different after the warehouse session. It took me a few days, but then I suddenly got it."

"Got what?" Alex asked.

"The cliques are breaking down. For years, I've noticed how employees eat together and stick together in their cliques, their clans, and their clubs. But something else is happening now. Our employees are mixing across the clans and the clubs, and the noise level in the lunchroom is higher than ever. So like any good HR type, I decided to investigate. Every day at lunch, I moved my tray around and listened in on the conversations."

"What did you learn?" Alex asked, his curiosity growing.

"People are talking about opportunities—opportunities to do good things in the company that can happen only with fuller cooperation from other clans and teams. So they are reaching out to both get and give help. We are becoming a community." Matt leaned forward and interlaced his fingers in front of him to demonstrate. "We are weaving together in a good way. You know, Alex, as your HR guy, I've been all about defining our competencies and building our culture."

"That's good," Alex encouraged, sensing that his friend was in a confessional mood.

"Good, you bet. But I was missing the key right in front of me. Genuine community connects competency and culture." He drew it on Alex's office whiteboard.

$$Competency \leftarrow Community \rightarrow Culture$$

"Community, catalyzed by the shared goal achievement discussions we're having, is actually putting individual competencies to work. And the work itself that's happening across functions, the giving and getting of help, is literally building the high-performance culture we have been hoping to create." Alex looked down at Matt's doodle.

"Do you mind if I keep this, Matt? I'd like to help you with this."

"I hoped that you would say that, Alex. By the way, you should see the lunchroom for yourself."

So at lunch, Alex went to see community in action. Just as described, animated, cross-clan discussions were everywhere. One group was eating while gathered around a product prototype. Alex recognized a couple of customers sitting at another lunchroom table, joining another product discussion.

Alex watched. He didn't want to intrude, and yet he wanted to help. *I guess I've tried to be the hero out in front, but perhaps I should be joining with them, to serve them—a serving leader.* He opened his brown-bag lunch and pulled out a sandwich. There on top was a handwritten note from Rachel.

Daddy,

I am happy that we are giving each other second chances. I need you, Dad.

Love you,
Rachel

Alex put the note back in his bag and lowered his head so that no one would see the emotion on his face. When he recovered, he scanned the room again. His eyes fell on a far corner, where Nate Strayer was having lunch with his controller and several other colleagues. This tight knot of managers stood out from the rest of the groups in the lunchroom.

If Alex could have listened in on this group, he would have heard a very interesting conversation.

Mike Miller, the company controller, was pushing back on his boss. "I hear what you're asking me to do, Nate. You know that I've spent a lot of energy in the last few weeks trying to manage the chaos. People are indeed overstepping the previous boundaries." He looked around the lunchroom. "They're running multiple budgets together, stopping and starting projects. But I have to say I think, on the whole, this is a good thing. This is why I got into finance in the first place. I wanted to help people shift gears, stop what's not working, and shift resources into the best opportunities. I don't just want to control; I want to *collaborate*."

Nate interrupted, pointing his finger forcefully at his subordinate. "You are a controller, for goodness' sake, Mike. You're not helping us; you're joining them." He slammed his glass on the table with enough force to nearly break it. Heads turned.

Mike said evenly, "This is not about us and them, Nate; this is about all of us."

As Nate's lunch mates finished and dispersed, Alex wheeled over to Nate. "Okay, my friend, let's get back to what's bothering you. Why does it seem like you want to jump out of your skin lately?"

Nate's response was calm, but he was clearly frustrated. "I just don't see this greater good—Greater Goal stuff. It's not realistic. I thought you and I agreed on process a long time ago. I thought that's why you brought me here. I want success for the company like you do. And I also want to get what I need for me and mine. I may not be high-minded, but at least I'm honest."

Alex drew a deep breath. "Can you honestly say you can't see the value of reaching for more for others?"

"Leave that to the Nelson Mandelas of the world. Shouldn't we be focused on keeping this company on track? How about just looking after our business so that the people here keep their jobs? Plus, what about our end game? I thought we agreed that when the time is right, we want this company to be an attractive acquisition."

"Nate, I'm not saying we shouldn't want to be known for high performance. But how we get there matters. And to what end? I'm thinking about how different our management decisions would be if we took into account the impact on our triple bottom line."

"Triple bottom line? You mean like social justice? Alex, isn't that above our pay grade?"

"Actually, I take the definition from Ken Blanchard in his book *Leading at a Higher Level*: provider of choice, employer of choice, and investment of choice. I'm starting to see how these all work together for high performance while aiming for high purpose. In fact, Nate, I'm starting to see this as the way to sustain real growth, a framework for all our decisions."

"Are you sure you're not making things more complicated than they need to be?"

"Not if it means doing the right thing and avoiding a mess like our friends across town got into," said Alex. Nate silently remembered a competitor's recent lawsuits. The company ignored its own surveillance of adverse product effects and caused untold patient suffering.

"I know you've been through a lot lately, Alex. Don't you think you should give your recovery more time before you make changes to Beckley?"

"Actually, I have never been so sure of myself. Or I should say I'm sure of this course of action. It's not about me any-more. I believe the people of this company have the ability to decide our future together. How about you, Nate? What would it take for you to commit to 'leading at a higher level,' as Blanchard would say?"

"Honestly, I'm not there, Alex. I get a sick feeling in the pit of my stomach when I think of getting advice from my staff about how to run accounting and finance."

"I can relate. I felt that way before the warehouse sessions. And the board may still drop me. But really, Nate, look inside and ask yourself what's underneath your issues with the ap-proach. There are people who want to help you."

Nate looked away. "Maybe."

Alex could see that the challenge was still there. "Let's talk again soon, Nate," said Alex as he rolled away.

Later that week, Alex was in his office, pondering Nate's remarks and wondering how others at Beckley were doing with commitment to the Greater Goal. Alex's assistant popped into his office. "Dr. Stan would like a minute with you. He is right outside."

"Please, come on in, Stan!" Alex called to the outer office.

Dr. Stan Ralston was the genius behind many of Beckley's most important patents. He was an early partner with Alex's dad. He walked in slowly, showing some unsteadiness. He sat down on Alex's couch as he had done a thousand times before with Alex's father.

"I've got some news for you, Alex—something I think you will like."

"Sure. What is it, Stan? I could use some good news."

"Your father always made it clear that our values, including 'do the right thing,' should always win out, even when the 'right thing' might cost us some money."

"So how do you think it's going, Stan?" Alex responded.

"We got a little off course recently."

"Ouch," Alex said. "I thought this was good news."

"It is," Dr. Stan continued. "The Greater Goal work is bringing us back into alignment with our higher values. Here's the story. Two of my engineers came to me with a situation. It seems that we were getting ready to produce the new multifunction monitor with some components that didn't exactly meet our quality standards, but the parts were amazingly cheap. They probably would not have failed immediately in high numbers. Their use would have added to our profit margin in the next few quarters—coincidentally, through bonus time," Dr. Stan raised his eyebrows, *"before* we had any real failures in the field."

"Are you getting to the good news?" Alex interrupted.

"Yes. After the warehouse session, the entire team came to me en masse with a change proposal. In light of our values and their discussions about them, they decided they could not put customers at risk. That's good."

"I agree," Alex said quizzically.

"And here's the added bonus: they reengineered the product, simplified it, and did away with the need for those parts completely! We have a higher quality, more reliable, and less expensive product on our hands now—all because our team *decided to do the right thing*. It's a win-win. Our recommitment to our own values led us to do the right thing. We got an even better, more profitable product. I just thought you'd want to hear this. I think we're getting our groove back, Alex. Values driven, like your old man," Dr. Stan said with a grin.

Alex smiled and sat back in his chair. "You're right. That is good news. Tell me when you have any more of those stories because I could sure use the encouragement."

Dr. Stan rocked a little bit forward on the couch. "Well if you're up for it, I have one more."

"Really?"

"Yes. I was going to save this one, but now is a good time."

"Go, Stan," Alex prompted.

"Well, we got a request in Research and Development—who knows how it filtered into us?—a special request from a mother. She didn't have anywhere else to go. She asked if we could modify one of our implantable cardiovascular devices for her son—actually, he's her only son. The normal devices just wouldn't work for his unique anatomy. So we, of course, looked at the technical problems. On the face of it, though, the modification was tough and cost prohibitive. Given all our design time, the new materials, and a one-time manufacturing, it would have been hundreds of thousands of dollars for this one device. So I turned down the request. But this mother, well, she was persistent. She actually came here to Pittsburgh and met with us and eventually got through to us. Alex, your dad would have done what we did." Dr. Stan pointed to the picture of Russ Beckley on Alex's bookshelf. "We decided to customize our basic model to make a one-of-a-kind device for this child. We worked on it on nights and weekends. I actually went up to Cleveland and participated in the surgery to put it in. It was perfect. I've got pictures of this sweet kid." With that, Stan showed Alex some pictures taken with his cell phone.

"And the rest of the story is good news. Along the way to designing, experimenting with, and redesigning this one device, we had to try a number of innovative approaches. A couple of these ideas really worked well. We are now pulling them into our main product line. Customers love what we're doing. So you know what, Alex? Again, doing the right thing is making money for us. Talk about a Greater Goal story. I'm sorry we didn't bring you in on this earlier, but the old Alex—"

Alex stopped him. "I know, but I love it, Stan. Keep up the good work." With that Stan stood, shook Alex's hand, thanked him, and walked out.

13. Greater Goal Coaching

Alex's assistant overheard the whole exchange with Dr. Stan and stepped back into Alex's office to comment, "Isn't that great? I do wish your dad was here to see that. By the way, Quinn is here to see you."

As Alex waited for Quinn to come in, he looked around his office. Posted on all four walls were enlarged pictures of the whiteboards from the warehouse sessions with the goals and initiative descriptions. Almost metaphorically they covered up many pieces of Alex's past accomplishments. He smiled to himself as he realized how much he appreciated the current office "artwork." Quinn joined him in his office and also noticed the new décor. "What do you think of what's happened, Alex?"

"Amazing," Alex answered. "I just had Dr. Stan in here giving me some great stories. Just amazing—I never knew there were so many great ideas and such great energy for our Greater Goal. I guess when you constantly just tell people what to do, you never really tap into the greatness that lies within them." His voice betrayed some sadness.

Quinn asked, "What's wrong, Alex?"

Alex answered thoughtfully, his voice almost fearful. "Old habits die hard, Quinn. I'm afraid the 'old me' is going to mess this up. I am not so sure of how to run the organization. What happens next?"

Quinn moved closer to Alex and looked at him with his eyes focused and resolute. "Alex, you were created with extraordinary gifts to do extraordinary things. Your father saw this." At the mention of his father, a lump rose in Alex's throat. "And I see this."

"I hope I can become the leader my father wanted me to be," Alex responded quietly.

"Remember when we said the key is that it's not about you?" Quinn asked. "Well, being a great leader means bringing out greatness in others, helping them develop their talents into strengths and success. With shared goals you are ensuring that everyone in the company is aligned and working together. But high-purpose–high-performance companies put in place a flywheel of achievement that combines *alignment* with *breakthrough*. Your people identified the Greater Goal and shared goals and then they designed initiatives they can commit to. Now help them accomplish those goals by sponsoring well-crafted initiatives. These initiatives link people across functions to reach the goals."

Quinn wrote on Alex's whiteboard.

1. Charter initiative teams to focus on shared goals and dramatic breakthrough success.

2. Ensure a great learning and development experience for the team members.

3. Implement a powerful coaching process and cascade that capability to all levels.

"I call this approach 'initiative-based development.' Project success and people development are achieved with a special kind of coaching capability. I called it 'Greater Goal Coaching.' Like a demonstration?"

"I am completely intrigued, Quinn."

Quinn smiled. "Great! I have some questions that could help you think through how you can make a great contribution to the company. And these are the kinds of questions that you can use to help others achieve their goals."

"Carry on!" replied Alex.

"To implement the shared goals that were created, what high-impact breakthroughs would radically advance Beckley toward its shared goals?"

The power of that question was the first thing Alex felt. *Man, Quinn can really frame a question. I could learn from that*, Alex thought. He offered a number of ideas while Quinn recorded them on the whiteboard.

"What else? What other ideas do you have?" asked Quinn. Alex added to the list. "Give me a few more, Alex," Quinn said, and then he asked, "What's another idea?" after Alex offered more.

At first, Alex thought Quinn was looking for a certain answer that he wanted Alex to come up with on his own. After a few more minutes, Alex realized that Quinn's prompts allowed Alex to fully investigate his own thinking. The variety of ideas that emerged was surprising. After about ten minutes, Alex pretended to wave a white flag and said with a smile, "Okay, Quinn, that's all I've got!"

Over the next hour, Quinn asked more compelling questions that engaged and motivated Alex's very best thinking, such as

- What bridges can you build to others to get their help in advancing the Greater Goal?
- What are the most persistent barriers that stand in the way?
- What actions would bust through these barriers and help you move toward success?
- What are the collective strengths of the individuals on your team?
- How will you deploy the strengths of your team members toward specific opportunities?
- What relationships, knowledge capital, experiences, goodwill, and other hard and soft assets could you use to create the breakthroughs better and faster?
- How will you gauge progress and continually improve along the way?

With each question, Quinn probed to get Alex's best ideas. Only when Alex stated he was out of ideas would Quinn ask, "May I offer a thought on this?" This was motivating to Alex on a few fronts: he saw that he was able to access Quinn's experience, and he was able to access his own good ideas first. And it felt good to know that the quality of his own ideas was strong enough that Quinn did not often have much to add.

Alex thought another question was on the way, but Quinn finally stopped.

"Wow, that was really powerful, Quinn. I can't believe what just happened."

"Say more," Quinn prompted.

"I feel like we just accomplished more in one hour in terms of quality of thinking than I have accomplished in weeks of work at Beckley."

Quinn smiled the smile of a teacher whose pupil had just discovered how to apply a theory. He then asked, "What did you notice, Alex, specifically about my role during our conversation?"

"Funny you should ask that—because it just struck me that you often go into a teaching mode when we are together. But this time you did not do that. Instead, you asked a lot of framing questions and I did most of the talking."

The smile of the teacher broadened.

"And you did offer some very relevant points, Quinn, and even asked my permission to do so."

"What do you think would have happened if I had offered my ideas first?" asked Quinn.

"I think I would have respected you as a great teacher and would have just gone with your thoughts." Alex smiled as the lightbulb fully came on. "And I never would have had to do the hard work of thinking for myself. The old me would have stopped after my first few thoughts, but those would not have had the deep impact of the answers that eventually showed up."

Quinn could no longer hide his teeth behind his grin. "There is greatness within you."

Alex nodded. "So now I guess you'll say my job is to go and help surface that greatness in others around me by being their thinking partner—as you just were to me."

"That is a great way to describe what we just practiced. This approach is critical for Greater Goal Coaching. It's different from other kinds of business or developmental coaching. This method aims to help others achieve the shared goals as guided by the Greater Goal and cascade the practice throughout the company." With that, Quinn drew the now-familiar Star Model on Alex's whiteboard.

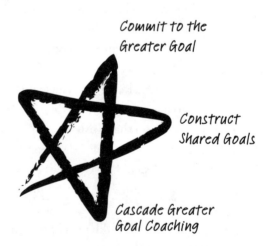

Commit to the
Greater Goal

Construct
Shared Goals

Cascade Greater
Goal Coaching

"The third practice is about helping all leaders, at every level of the company, coach their teams to achieve crucial shared goals. In my research on high-purpose–high-performance organizations, I noticed that the leaders were practicing something uniquely effective. They were doing something I could only describe as 'Greater Goal Coaching.'

"Here is what I saw these coaches doing—you've just experienced some of it. They coached their teams to target high-impact breakthroughs to radically advance toward the Greater Goal. Then these leaders coached their teams to engage with cross-functional partners to create success. They were coaching *bridge building*. These leaders inventoried the collective strengths of their teams and called on each and every person to help create breakthroughs. They also inventoried their teams' relationships, knowledge capital, experiences, and goodwill— hard and soft assets they could build upon to create breakthroughs better and faster. This was coaching by *building on strengths and assets*. Leaders coached their teams to seek out, analyze, and destroy the barriers that stood in the way of breakthroughs. These included all sorts of ideas and ways of working that actually worked against the Greater Goal: culture, methods, tools, training, teamwork, creativity, and even styles of leadership. They were coaching *barrier busting*.

"Finally, leaders coached their teams to conduct effective after-action reviews. They reflected on their success in creating breakthroughs to learn from what worked and what did not. They created learning experiences and then coached their teams to improve their approaches based on that learning. And they challenged the underlying theories that did not work and adopted new assumptions as needed. They were *building learning teams*.

"Greater Goal Coaching is the key to the implementation of shared goals. As I said, a Greater Goal Coach is doing a different sort of coaching." Quinn checked his watch and motioned toward the door. "Do you have a moment to roll down to Kevin's office?"

Kevin was expecting them. His desk was clean except for a pair of very old football shoes and a clump of metal lying next to them. "Looks like a pair of football cleats," said Alex.

Quinn asked Alex, "Do you know the Greek word *paraclete*?"

"Quinn, you are terrible!" Kevin chuckled, mentally chalking up a win for Quinn in their friendly "worst comedy" competition.

"I'll admit, pretty bad," Quinn replied. "But hear me out. *Paraclete*, in Greek, means 'advocate' or 'helper'—one who comes alongside another in accomplishing a task or goal. A paraclete acts as a guide and resource in the business sense, a 'thinking partner,' as you said, Alex.

"Greater Goal Coaching is not telling or teaching. It's about drawing ideas and answers out of those who have them but just need a guide or a thinking partner to help them.

"May I share another pocket card with you, Alex?"

"Of course, Quinn. I would be disappointed if you were not prepared for the moment!"

Practice Three: Cascade Greater Goal Coaching

Principles:

- Aim for breakthroughs.
- Build bridges and break through barriers.
- Build on strengths, assets, and success.
- Create learning teams and be a thinking partner.

"Kevin," Alex ventured, pointing at the cleats, "mind if I hang on to these for a while?"

"Keep them, Alex. I wore those in college before I was with the pros. Let the cleats be a reminder of Greater Goal Coaching and a reminder of how difficult getting traction for change can be."

14. Reinforcing Alignment

After work, Quinn drove Alex to his favorite local restaurant, a chic place called "Casbah." Once they were back in Alex's neighborhood, Quinn strolled and Alex hobbled through Frick Park, just around the corner from Alex's house.

Alex got to the point. "I have to deal with Nate. I think I knew from the beginning that this was coming. How do I do the right thing?" The men walked and talked about the situation with Nate.

After a while Quinn steered the conversation in another direction. "Alex, I wish I could tell you Nate is the only problem you have, or that you will ever face, on your journey to a Greater Goal. *Hidden in your company are forces that will undermine the hard-fought alignment you have gained.* Every company culture has built-in rewards that work in opposition to alignment to the Greater Goal. Identifying and defusing this opposition is critical to achieving ongoing alignment." He pulled a small card from his back pocket and handed it to Alex. Upon unfolding it, Alex looked upon another hand-drawn star with a new practice added.

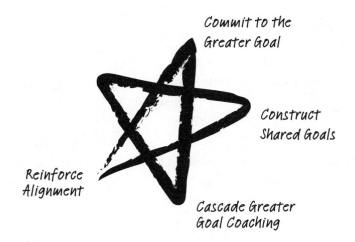

Commit to the
Greater Goal

Construct
Shared Goals

Reinforce
Alignment

Cascade Greater
Goal Coaching

"Reinforce alignment? What does that mean?"

"Let's rest your leg for a moment. Grab a bench. Alex, dozens of hidden forces can pull people out of alignment. If you learn to spot and counter these forces, you can reinforce alignment to the Greater Goal. I can offer you some perspectives, like lenses, for you to see these forces. The first lens is this: people will align to what they really value, really treasure. Many people in the company genuinely value the Greater Goal, but day-to-day pressure from other rewards will compete for their hearts."

"For instance?"

"*Hidden rewards* are right now reinforcing behavior not aimed at the Greater Goal. There are rewards for activity instead of achievement, rewards for playing it safe versus taking risk and innovating, rewards for competition versus collaboration, rewards for taking credit versus giving credit, rewards for accomplishing easy goals versus stretching for breakthrough goals, and many others." Alex nodded his understanding, and Quinn went on.

"You also have to learn to see through the *'culture lens.'* Culture is real, you know. Like the wind, you can't see it, but you can see its effects. The culture of the company can push people out of alignment when it reinforces doing good things that are actually the enemy of great things. Here are some cultural values I've noted at Beckley that promote good over great." Alex took notes as Quinn talked:

- *Problem solvers* are valued over *opportunity seekers.*
- *"Make the bottom line"* stands in the way of *"invest for the long run."*
- *"Leaders are the ones in charge"* stands in the way of *"leadership is a team sport."*
- *"We need to recruit the best talent"* stands in the way of *"we need systems that help our current talent perform at their very best."*

"Shall I go on?" Quinn asked.

"Maybe a couple more. These are great though, Quinn. I see how the short-term *good* gets in the way of the possibility for long-term *great.*"

"Here's one more cultural element that I have heard expressed at Beckley," Quinn said. "It is *'that's the way we've always done it here'* versus *'let's try a new approach.'*"

"Ouch. I've used that first expression myself. But isn't 'the way we have always done it' building on the success of the past? And that's a good thing, right?"

"Yes, Alex, but only if that way continues to be validated by a thorough after-action review. If a process and its results are consistent with your values and prove to be truly useful in achieving your Greater Goal, then definitely do more of that."

"I've got the rewards and culture lenses. Do you have a third lens?"

"Indeed I do," Quinn responded. "*Turf*. Turf is the greatest opponent of alignment to the Greater Goal. Turf is in effect when you hear '*my* department, *my* team, *my* budget' and a win-lose outcome is tolerated." Quinn looked up with a smile. "It's as silly as saying, 'I'm glad it's *your* half of the boat that's sinking!' Alex, you have a good bit of turf in your company."

"You really know how to encourage a guy, don't you, Quinn?" Alex asked as he began to rise on his crutches.

"Yes, I want to encourage you—that is, to help you to find the 'courage' needed to contend with the opponents of alignment," said Quinn.

"Okay then, coach, where do we start?"

"Where do you see the most pervasive barriers to alignment, Alex, based on what we've gone over?"

"I guess I'd start with the serious turf issues." Alex stood, stumbled, and flailed to regain his balance.

Quinn continued, "You started to tackle turf by asking the entire company to create shared goals. Now that change is underway, you can continue the momentum by decisively defeating the 'Turf Monster' in an important area. Pick one of the projects you brainstormed about during our Greater Goal Coaching session. Help your people win the turf war."

"No question," Alex quickly responded. "I'd pick *new product development*. We discussed how crucial it was and how little progress we've made. New product development includes early market research, engineering, manufacturing, sales and marketing, and customer feedback. It's a full cycle.

Since I arrived at Beckley, the new-product-development process has been a bitter battle of finger-pointing and a lot of 'us versus them' and 'it's their fault.'"

"That's the Turf Monster, for sure. So," Quinn challenged, "how would you realign those silos you just named?"

Alex stopped walking and hung on his crutches. "You are asking *me*? Well, I guess I would draw a completely new boundary around all the silos and put in place a multifunctional team. I'd include them all—research and development, engineering, manufacturing, marketing, and sales, all together. If I could dream big, I'd put them all together in their own physical space, wrap them around an important new project, and challenge them to make it work."

"Do it," Quinn said. "Do you have a product in mind now?"

"Actually, I do!" Alex said, looking down at his own busted leg. "It's a product I have a stake in. Quinn, I need to regrow bone. Stuck somewhere in our pipeline is a product that could help me. We call it the 'Bone OSA Stimulator,' or 'BOS' for short."

"Why do you guys have so many acronyms?" Quinn laughed out loud. "Everything is a TLA with you guys."

"What's that?" It was Alex's turn to be confused.

"TLA is a three-letter acronym that stands for . . . 'Three-Letter Acronym,'" Quinn said, and laughed at his own joke. "Do just what you have in your mind."

They walked back to Alex's house and sat in rocking chairs on his wide front porch. He and Quinn sketched out a plan. In the growing twilight, neighbors saw two gentlemen waving their arms, painting a picture that only they could see.

✡

The next day, Alex and his HR vice president, Matt Joachim, met with Nate in Alex's office. As soon as they had settled into chairs, Alex got to the point.

"Nate, we're friends, and I respect you and appreciate all that you've done for me and for Beckley. But you've made it clear that you don't agree with what's going on here as of late."

Nate shook his head. "Not entirely."

"I'd like you to take a few days off to think about what you really want, where this company is headed, and whether you want to be a part of that."

Nate's eyebrows rose. "That sounds fatal."

"Not fatal. But this is a choice point," Alex said.

"I see," Nate said. "In that case, I'll see you next Monday. Have a good week, gentlemen."

That afternoon, Alex gathered the senior team in the conference room. Dan Meyers heard about the meeting and invited himself. *Unusual for Dan to be here,* Alex thought. *Is this another test?* Alex pushed the negative thought out of his head and addressed his colleagues.

"Let's get going. Nate is taking off the rest of the week on a personal matter."

Questioning looks appeared around the room, but the truth was that no one was surprised. Alex called them to task. "I know we're all pretty excited about the alignment that we see emerging around the company, but I suggest there are reward, cultural, and turf forces at work in the company that can sabotage our alignment. Let's talk about all of that honestly."

There were a lot of nods around the table, so Alex pressed on. *"Why don't we name some of the opponents to alignment together and create an action plan to address them."* The team proceeded to brainstorm a list.

Opponents of Alignment to Our Greater Goal

Opponent of Alignment	Action for Reinforcing Alignment
Our goal system is focused on individual performance.	Emphasize shared goals that align us.
Our budgeting process emphasizes single-unit performance.	Allocate money for cross-department "joint ventures" and encourage midyear modifications to the budgets to pursue emerging opportunities.
Sales regions compete with each other.	Build up our total sales force rewards for overall achievements.
We have multiple pet product-development projects.	Use strategic product-development road maps and say no to projects that don't meet strategic criteria.
We tolerate finger-pointing and blaming of other teams and divisions when things go wrong.	Build and promote a Shared Goal Achievement Process that facilitates collaboration.
We promote leaders based on individual achievements.	Promote leaders based mostly on how they create shared success.

And the last action item, which they all agreed to, was "We are going to continue to find and defeat the other hidden opponents of alignment in our company."

At this point, Quinn's head was cocked down and he was doodling, half listening to the tail end of the conversation and half concentrating on his drawing. Alex snuck a look.

Invisible   Opposition

Quinn flipped the card over. On the back was this:

Practice Four: Reinforce Alignment

Principles:

- Radical commitment is reserved for what we truly treasure.
- Alignment is opposed by mostly invisible forces. Make them visible and defeat them.

Alex smiled and then moved to his idea for a new-product-development "venture team." Alex suggested that the cross-functional team be formed under Mikala Whales. The venture team was chartered, and Mikala quickly recruited members from across the functions of research and development, engineering, manufacturing, marketing, sales, human resources, and finance.

The group was cross-functional, determined, and ready to roll by the end of the week.

When Nate arrived at work the following Monday morning, he handed Alex a letter of resignation. "You are right, this isn't for me," he said.

"Thank you, Nate," he said, "for your courage."

"It doesn't take much courage to jump from a burning ship. Good luck, Alex."

Mikala and the new-product-development venture team immediately moved into an unused space on the Beckley campus. A colorful flag, like the kind climbers plant after a successful summit assault, appeared immediately on the floor. It was a sign of the adventure going on inside and of great things to come. At the end of the week, Mikala sent Alex an e-mail with a cryptic subject line: "10× then 100× in Pursuit of the Greater Goal."

"Can you explain, face to face?" Alex wrote back.

Within minutes she was explaining the formula in person to Alex. "We hope to hit project milestones at ten times the speed of previous teams. We want to have one hundred times more impact on customers than any previous project. We are aiming at '10× then 100×.'"

"Okay then. Wow!" Alex said.

"We know we will get there," Mikala responded with a mischievous grin. "This is us," she said and then mimicked a Quinn drawing on Alex's whiteboard.

We Are   Aligned!

"Keep me updated. Let me help with barrier busting and bridge building if I can," said Alex. "I am working on my Greater Goal Coaching skills and sponsorship role."

The next person in Alex's office was Quinn. He spotted Mikala's drawing on the whiteboard. "Nice! You see, my doodles are catching on. Are you ready for more Greater Goal Coaching?"

"Absolutely." Just then Kevin Jordan stuck his head in. Seeing Quinn in the room, he said, "Sorry to interrupt," and started to back out.

"Oh, no, join us." Alex waved him in. "We are just doing some reflecting. It's a 'coaching' thing," he said, using his fingers to make quotation marks. "Ha!"

"I'd be glad to. Sort of like reviewing game film?"

"Yes, it is—game film review," said Quinn.

Alex turned serious and started the conversation. "Before we actually dig in, gentlemen, I just want to say thank you both for conspiring together for my second chance. I figured it out—you plotted together to help me."

"You're welcome," Quinn and Kevin responded together. "Truth be told," Kevin continued, "it was your father who recruited us to help you if you ever made it back to Beckley."

"But he didn't know I would even come back."

"He had hopes," Quinn assured him. "And he planned for your return." Quinn chose the moment to return to Greater Goal Coaching. "So, Kevin, Alex and I have been doing some reflecting on the opponents of alignment. I was just getting ready to ask Alex how he, himself, may have contributed to the lack of alignment. What has become clearer to you, Alex?"

Alex chuckled to himself and admitted, "In the words of one of my Air Force Academy friends, before my accident I was 'all thrust and no rudder.' I pushed with high expectations and high pressure. Now I'm relying on alignment to the Greater Goal to unleash and direct more energy than I could have summoned with my command-and-control leadership."

Kevin jumped in, "Gee, that reminds me of my last Super Bowl season."

Alex and Quinn both groaned together in good humor. "Not another Super Bowl story!"

"Okay, okay, I'll let you off this one time," Kevin remitted. "Still, alignment, team spirit, and dedication are familiar to me. Shared leadership, what we call 'serving leadership,' is what it takes to win championships. See the similarity?" Kevin asked Alex.

"Well, actually I do. Shared goals and shared leadership help teams form across functional lines. Not unlike a great sports team. I see that overfocusing on individual goals actually drove down overall performance—'goals gone wild.' Shared goals tied to good strategies and well-designed initiatives enable company-wide performance."

The three men continued talking for another hour. Finally, Alex's assistant walked in with her hands on her hips to announce, "Alex, and the rest of you, you've gone way over on time. You've got another meeting."

Getting ready for bed late that evening, Alex noticed that something was different about his room. Someone had changed the sheets and placed a new quilt on his bed. He looked closer. There was also a note on his pillow—in Rachel's handwriting:

Tomorrow is cooking night—be ready!

I love you, Dad,

Rachel

15. Dinner and a Guest

Saturday at last! Alex and Rachel were cooking—their third Saturday feast together. This time it was to be Italian like Mom used to make. In their warm, country-style kitchen, the two wore matching red-and-white checked aprons. The ingredients were laid out on the center island in an orderly fashion—at least on Alex's side. On Rachel's side, the ingredients were laid out more "creatively." Rachel read from the recipe. She added her own impromptu suggestions as they went along. Grandma stayed in the background, only coaching when she thought there was a threat of serious injury.

Beside the stove, Rachel had propped up pictures of her mother. "I want Mom to be part of this," she said. In forty-five minutes the kitchen resembled a sort of expressionist painting. Colorful ingredients were splashed about on the counters and on the cooks. A daughter's "improv" was meeting with a father's "deliberate approach." Somewhere in the middle, something marvelous was happening.

Just then, the doorbell rang. Alex wandered through the foyer to the front door. He opened it, and there he was—John J. Williams, the man they'd encountered when leaving the co-op!

John's hair was neatly combed, and he had on a nice suit. Alex recognized the cut and quality of Armani. *What is he doing wearing that?* he wondered. And then, *What is he doing here?*

Alex was standing with his mouth open when his daughter came to see who had arrived. For the second time, Rachel took charge. "Mr. Williams! I'm so glad you came! You can help."

Sidestepping Alex, John followed Rachel into the kitchen. "Please call me John," he said as he was introduced to Annie, who warmly shook his hand.

"Welcome to our home, John," she said.

Then John went to work like he knew his way around a kitchen. He also set the table perfectly. Alex thought with certainty. *He's done this before somewhere.*

With multiple trips from the kitchen to the dining room, the meal was placed on the long, antique table. John looked up at the European ceiling that Alex's father had imported. John remarked, "That reminds me of a ceiling I saw once in Heidelberg."

"Germany?" asked Alex.

"Yes. Heidelberg, Germany. I studied there."

"Can we say grace?" Rachel asked, immediately taking John's hand in her own and her father's on the other side. "Dad, you pray."

John joined the family, reverently bowing his head, repeating the family's familiar prayer word for word. Then they dug in.

The meal was marvelous. Every dish worked. The spices that Rachel had insisted upon were evident and amazing. Over the meal, they heard John's story. John had lost his job in the "Great Recession." He looked down at his plate—or rather through it, it seemed.

"I started drinking," he admitted, "and eventually wound up on the streets." He looked up. "I'm in a twelve-step program. It's working. I'm ashamed of myself for asking you for change."

"Nothing to be ashamed of," Alex said, now engaging. "Where are you living?"

"I'm at a shelter downtown, part of Living Ministries. I get meals, donated clothing, and a whole lot of love."

"Tell me more about the people who come to the shelter and how the program works," Alex encouraged.

So John did. He went on to describe a greater love that got through to him. "It's an amazing community to be a part of," he said. "And not just for people in my situation but for the staff and volunteers too. It's changing all of our lives."

Rachel looked thoughtful. "You know that Greater Goal stuff we've been talking about, Dad?" Alex knew something good was coming. "Well, maybe cooking this meal and meeting John is part of a bigger plan. Maybe we could, you know, go down to the shelter that John's talking about and do some cooking."

"We don't see many young girls at the shelter—the program is for homeless men," John said, sounding doubtful.

"No, that's exactly the kind of place for a girl like me," Rachel disagreed. "Don't you think, Dad?" She looked over at Alex for support.

"You bet, Rachel. John, you don't know who you're dealing with here," Alex said, and everyone laughed. "Let's go down to Living Ministries together, Rachel," Alex offered. "We can find out if they can use some volunteer cooks or whatever . . . they may not like my cooking."

John shrugged and laughed at the way father and daughter were obviously testing the water with each other. More and more, John felt comfortable and curious with these newfound friends. "So . . . who can tell me more about this 'Greater Goal' stuff?"

16. Building on Success

Promising to share the *fifth and final practice* of high-purpose–high-performance organizations, Quinn had picked Alex up for a ride in his restored 1968 black Chevy Corvette. After a cruise through the East End, making their way to the downtown freeway interchanges, Quinn and Alex were soon roaring up the wide-open interstate between Pittsburgh and Cleveland.

"I actually talked to you about this next organization way back when I first met you. You are going to love it! By the way, Alex, I hear that you got John J. Williams an interview at Beckley. Good idea."

Alex noted the small curve of a smile on Quinn's face as the Corvette accelerated with a deep rumble. "You like driving this, don't you?" Alex asked the obvious.

"Oh yeah," Quinn responded, mimicking an American accent and response. "I love the drive over to my client, the Cleveland Wellness Network—it gives me a chance to get out the 'Vette." He grinned. "It's classic American muscle.

"Driving is one of my favorite things to do. When I was growing up in Scotland, my dad was a traveling minister. He had a red MG-B convertible. I loved our time in the car, just the two of us being buddies. Mom said it was a questionable car for a preacher, but I think she really loved how much he enjoyed it. And on those drives my dad listened to me, really gave me all his attention. Maybe that's why I love to drive."

The two men sat quietly for a while, enjoying the ride. Alex broke the spell. "What am I going to see at the Wellness Network?"

"The fifth practice," said Quinn, "is to *build on success*." He handed Alex a card from his shirt pocket.

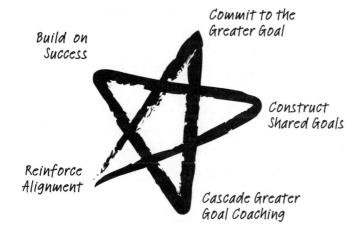

"You're getting alignment of goal and purpose in the organization. Now you can rev up performance." He punched the accelerator a little to make his point. *"You do this by spotting and building on the success you are achieving throughout the company."*

"Cool," said Alex, holding on to his seat.

Quinn continued. "Anyway, it starts with looking for what is already going well in your organization, looking for even the faintest signals of success.

"I like the saying '*Future high performance is already here; it is just unevenly distributed.*' Significant success is already quietly happening at Beckley Medical. This fifth practice is about identifying potential breakthroughs and reinforcing those quiet successes. Napoleon did this, you know. At the beginning of a battle, he would deploy a group of drummers along the front line. When a breakthrough in the enemy's lines occurred anywhere along the battlefront, the nearest drummer was instructed to beat his drum loudly, and the rest of the troops were taught to wheel around and pour into the breakthrough—capitalizing on success."

"Will I see this at the Cleveland Wellness Network?" Alex asked.

"Yes," Quinn said. "Today you're going to meet with Dr. Tony Phillips, the CEO. He will show you how the Wellness Network makes rapid progress all across the enterprise toward its strategic goals. The Wellness Network is an impressive $9 billion a year hospital system, as well as a world-class research and teaching enterprise."

"Tell me about Tony."

"He is not easily defined. He says he's not just leading a company; he's leading a *cause*. This man won a medal for heroism, completed over twenty thousand heart surgeries, and is acknowledged by peers and patients as one of the finest surgeons in the world."

"Must have been an interesting journey from surgeon to CEO," mused Alex.

"Definitely," Quinn said emphatically. "Ahead of health-care reform, the people of the Wellness Network saw the need to change themselves earlier than most. They went through a top-to-bottom conversion to shared leadership, called here 'Serving Leadership.'"

"I read it on the website," Alex said.

"Good," replied Quinn. "But then they also decided that if they really were committed to the Greater Goal, they were going to change from an already successful model to something new."

Quinn flipped his signal light on, easing the Corvette onto an Interstate 480 exit ramp.

"So, Alex, what you're also going to see at the Wellness Network is an amazing organization that has reinvented itself by building on success."

They pulled into an ultramodern parking structure in the midst of dozens of medical buildings. It was a stunning campus—a mini medical city. Within minutes, they were through a walkway tunnel and outside Tony's office. While Alex was still admiring the art in an outer office, Quinn rapped on the slightly open door to Tony's office.

"This is where I leave you, Alex. We'll meet up again after lunch. I'm involved with several different groups of entrepreneurs and other individuals in pursuit of their own Greater Goals. One such group is right here in the city. See you after lunch."

Tony's door opened, and the man himself stood before Alex. His handshake was powerful. "So, Alex, Quinn put us together. He's a good man." Quinn acknowledged the compliment and waved good-bye. "I also knew your father—he was a friend and a good leader. I hear you are like him." Alex blushed and wondered if he would meet Tony's standards too.

Like the exterior of the hospital grounds, the office's interior was cutting-edge contemporary in design and sparse. *Very Zen-like*, Alex thought. The office was undoubtedly high-tech, but the centerpiece of Tony's table contained dozens of sharpened pencils. *A touch of old school.*

"Thank you for your time," Alex started.

Tony waved his hand as if to say the time was not a sacrifice. "Glad to show you what we have here," he said. "I can't claim a lot of credit. I'm still learning on the job. They don't exactly teach you how to lead a large enterprise in medical school, you know."

"Quinn says you're pretty good at *building on success*."

Tony sat back. "As clinicians, we have all trained to be problem solvers. But this is not about problem solving. This is about innovation, opportunity, and possibility. Let me show you what I mean," Tony said and stood up. "We're going to have to walk for you to see what's happening here. Are you up for a walk?" Before Alex had a chance to respond, Tony was out the door—fast. He barely slowed his pace for Alex's cane-supported hobble. They entered a maze of halls and corridors, Tony confidently guiding them through.

Tony was talking the whole time. "When I reflect back on my surgical career, it is clear to me that from operation number one to operation twenty-some thousand, my team and I were constantly learning and innovating. Here, every day at the Network, we have thousands of innovations occurring simultaneously all over the place. If I could identify and capture the genuine breakthroughs that were occurring across the enterprise, amplify them, reinforce them, and do that every day, then we would have a *success* machine on our hands."

Tony's enthusiasm and confidence in the organization were unfaltering. "We encourage our leaders to scan across the entire organization for signs of unexpected success that advance us toward our Greater Goal."

Tony pulled a small notepad from his suit pocket and began to sketch, just like Quinn was always doing. He showed his picture to Alex.

Scan for Signs of Success

"Our leaders constantly scan for successes anywhere in the Network," said Tony. "When we find something that works, we advertise it and encourage others to adopt it. We are focused on scaling up methods that make a difference."

Alex pulled out his own pen and notepad. "Can you give me your steps?"

"Sure," Tony replied. "I keep it all on a card. Got the habit from Quinn. Have one." He handed a printed card to Alex.

How to Be a Success Spotter and
Success Replicator

- Relentlessly search for innovations and unexpected successes.
- Root out the reasons and the process behind the success.
- Look for places to replicate the success at a greater scale.
- Reward both innovators and replicators.
- Repeat the cycle.

Alex asked, "You said 'unexpected successes'?"

"Yes. We expect projects to be successful and we look to build on that success. But there is also a subtle little bump in margin, an improvement in a patient's experience, more engagement in a unit, or better clinical results. The observant leader spots faint signals of success that indicate something new. The leader goes after the root cause of that success, replicates the new thinking and the practice, and tries to increase the scope and scale."

Tony resumed their tour and eventually led Alex into a room where an executive sat behind a forest of computer screens. "Yuan, tell Alex what you are up to, why, and what you're going to do next."

Dr. Yuan Lee didn't even hesitate at the multipart question. He stood up and shook Alex's hand.

"We noticed something about our patients," he said. "Many of them were coming to us armed with their own stacks of Internet articles on their disease, paper medical records, and lots of other disorganized information. And when they left, they wanted even more information and the latest research on their disease state, and in general wanted to stay in touch with the Wellness Network.

"A couple of our IT staff built something on their own to help with this. They built the coolest, next-generation, consumer-friendly, electronic medical record 'lite' system from scratch in a skunk-works operation. We did some inexpensive pilot testing, starting small. We had good success on a small scale. Next we partnered with a very well-known electronic medical records company to scale up the system and integrate it into that company's own platform. We made it secure and accessible. It's even available on iPhones and that BlackBerry of yours."

"Yes," Alex acknowledged, "I love my little 'Berry. You could say it changed my life."

Yuan didn't pick up on the subtext behind Alex's statement but smiled anyway. He then gave Alex a ten-minute tutorial, with Tony standing by and looking satisfied, on the approaches his department was testing online. "We could use this," Alex noted. "Do you need a distribution partner?" he asked Tony.

"We can look into it," Tony promised. "Yuan, could you follow up? And now, Alex, there's more to see. Let's go." Tony was a man comfortable with being in charge and charging people up.

As they headed down a new corridor, Tony prepared Alex for the next stop. "There is another venture that illustrates our commitment to building on success particularly well," Tony said. "I asked two of the principal innovators to meet with us today."

As they entered an elevator to ascend to another floor, Tony said, "Part of building on success is taking what works for you *internally* and offering it to others *externally*. The case in point is with our wellness initiative in our employee health plan. We had great results improving the health of our own employees and families through our own innovative methods. We now hope to offer this model to the world."

With that, the group entered into the office of the chief human resources executive, Joe Paternuski, and the head of the employee health plan, Dr. Paul Tolinsky—or "Joe P. and Dr. T.," as Tony introduced them. "These two are leaders responsible for building on the success of our wellness initiative. Guys, Alex wants to hear our story about the Wellness Venture."

Joe P. shared first. Alex noted that this powerfully built executive looked more like a linebacker than an HR guy. "We didn't start out to commercialize a wellness offering. We started out several years back to do something good for our sixty thousand employees and their families. We are self-insured. We wanted to do something extra special for our own."

Dr. T. chimed in then. "So we took a deep dive into the best practices for keeping people well and preventing disease. We offered free access to exercise clubs and dieting groups, disease management, financial incentives, behavioral counseling, web links to resources, and we seriously addressed diabetes and obesity. And it all worked! Collectively we lost tens of thousands of pounds and people got healthier. Our employees and their families loved it. We got better clinical results and reduced total cost."

With every comment, Alex's eyes grew wider. "Wow!" he said when Dr. T. paused.

Joe P. picked back up again. "In keeping with our commitment to build on success, it became clear to us that we had something too good to keep to ourselves. We had something that could help people get healthier. Not what you would expect from an HR guy, huh?"

Dr. T. stepped in. "We now hope to offer all of this to companies, insurers, government health plans, and consumers."

"And I couldn't be happier," Tony broke in.

"Thanks," Alex said, "for sharing that with me. I'm completely impressed."

"You bet," Joe P. said, "Come see us anytime. By the way, I hear you have Kevin Jordan on your team. He was a great pro, but I think I took a few chunks out of him in college. Ask him about 'meeting' Joe P."

On the way back to Tony's office, they made a dozen detours. Tony stopped by various offices and workstations to hear about innovations and the latest successes. Purposefully wandering through the maze-like lab (Alex was lost), Tony observed and commented: "We are getting 20 percent off turnaround time on these lab tests. Can we scale that up across other tests? Show me how—run it through the screens, see if it scales, and don't give up if this can be big."

As Tony engaged with different people and ideas, Alex tried to give him confidential distance. Tony continued to draw him back in, asking for his opinions on issues and topics that Alex would be familiar with.

When they neared Tony's office again at last, Alex sighed, "Phew! Do you do that sort of thing a lot? We must have talked with a dozen people!"

"Yes," Tony said. "I love it! We all do this—not just me." Tony pulled out what looked like large family photo albums. He pointed to pictures of housekeepers, nurses, physicians, security guards, construction workers, and scores of other employees. "These are all 'Building on Success' champions. Because of them, we have one of the most patient-safe, innovative, and healing environments in the world. We aim to bend the healthcare cost curve and deliver world-class care. We are all caregivers here, you know." Alex was startled by this familiar phrase.

Tony looked up from the album at Alex. "By the way, we have a few ideas on how you could build on the success we are having using your own products. Care to hear?"

"Oh, yes," Alex responded, his excitement hard to repress.

"Then let's meet again," said Tony, "and bring some of your new-product-development people. And here—Quinn asked me to give you this card." Tony handed over a card with a smile and another crushing handshake.

Practice Five: Build on Success

Principles:

- *Search for what's working and scale it up.*
- *Create a culture of innovation in pursuit of the Greater Goal.*

17. No Man Is an Island

The next morning, Alex hobbled into the kitchen. Rachel and his mom were huddled around the kitchen bar with the TV news on quietly. Alex had a flashback to the morning of his accident, which seemed like ages ago.

"Good morning to my two favorite girls," he said.

Rachel looked up. "Oh, Dad, I have an idea for us."

Alex smiled. "What is it?"

"I was riding home on the bus yesterday, talking with one of my friends. I told her how much we enjoyed cooking together and how we wanted to do even more. Well, she's the one who had the idea. She and her dad are involved right here in Pittsburgh in the Urban Kitchen Project. It sounds perfect for us."

Alex poured his tea and sat down next to Rachel and his mother. "What is it?"

"The Urban Kitchen Project is about good, healthy food and cooking. It's right up our alley," Rachel said, smiling. "It started with a community farm in a city neighborhood. The original idea was to help lower-income families get access to healthy foods. Did you know our city neighborhoods are a food desert? That means grocery stores are not in the neighborhoods—just fast food. But then my friend's dad and some others noticed that even though these families could now get healthy food, they weren't really using it. Like us, Dad, they needed to learn how to cook with good fresh food.

"The Urban Kitchen Project is offering cooking classes each month to families right here near us. They're going to be learning to cook . . . well, here's the list." With that, Rachel pulled a sheet out of her backpack. "Mexican menu featuring fresh salsa and vegetarian burritos, soul food, stone soup for kids, and even learning how to can fresh veggies. We could join the group to improve our cooking skills but also to learn how we can pitch in at the Urban Kitchen Project. We're getting to be such good cooks anyway, and you know helping others learn how to cook and eat healthy . . . well, that sounds like progress toward a real Greater Goal. Don't you think so, Dad?"

Alex's mom said, "This time I want in too. I'd love to come along and help. How about the three of us getting involved?"

Rachel said, "I'll call my friend and ask her and her dad to stop by. Would tonight be okay?"

Alex could see that the two females had been plotting. He simply smiled. "I love it. And I will be working at home today. Dan suggested that I not attend the board meeting today." His tight grin showed that he was worried and trying not to show it.

Across town, Beckley's board of directors was meeting to deliberate the question of Alex's fitness to become the CEO

of Beckley Medical. Quinn and Kevin were called in to advise
the board. Quinn knew the board members were still divided
in their support for Alex. The vote was yet unclear. Dan Myers
sat in the middle of the long conference table, typically refus-
ing to sit at the head of the table. That spot was always left
empty.

Quinn shared first. "Alex has changed and grown. He's car-
rying out the work that Russ Beckley started."

Kevin spoke next. "Alex has taken us to the next level. He is
one among us, not above us—a first among equals. He is the
team captain." Kevin tapped his Super Bowl ring on the table.
He had worn it to make this point.

One of the board members, Celia Lev, spoke next. "Alex
and I were in the same MBA class. Alex was top of the class, a
real go-getter. But success was always about promoting himself. How much could he really change?"

Quinn responded with sincerity, "I believe his change is
genuine."

Dan leaned forward. "We're all glad that Alex came home.
But neither I nor Russ Beckley, if he were here, would promote him if it was not good for the company. We have a great
stewardship responsibility. So with that in mind, here is what
I believe . . . "

In what had been his bedroom for six months, but was
now again a family den, Alex reflected on the journey so far.
How differently he saw things now. What had been a desper-
ate, frantic drive to accomplish, perform, and succeed had
become eagerness to see where the next breakthroughs and

innovations would take this company. And he had a yearning
to be part of the community that Beckley was becoming—to
be useful in writing its future story. Alex looked up at his dad's
picture—despite his flaws, he had been a man of such high
purpose and performance. "What would you say to me, Dad?
Am I doing well? Am I doing good?"

A peaceful mood came over Alex. He was content with any
decision the board might give him. On his computer screen,
he pulled up an image of the star encircled by the five practices. Nicely drawn by a team member from Marketing, the
design had become a well-known icon throughout Beckley.

If Alex were to lead Beckley Medical, the Greater Goal
would still be his North Star. And more than that, he wanted
to continue his journey to become a different kind of leader—
a Serving Leader. He knew he wanted the CEO role, but did
he deserve it?

Just then the phone rang. Alex picked it up and heard the familiar Scottish brogue. "Do you have time tomorrow to go for a spin?" Quinn asked. His voice also betrayed fatigue and some emotion Alex could not name. It was not like Quinn.

"For you, always," Alex said, puzzled. "What do you have in mind?"

"I'd like to revisit the warehouse. It's important to me."

"Then let's go. Let me drive this time," Alex said. "I'll pick you up."

That night there was a storm. The air still felt heavy and damp the next morning. Alex leaned lightly on his cane as he approached his car. He sat for a minute before pulling out of the garage, remembering when he had paused there on the morning of his accident. *This is my big day . . . I'll hear from the board.* He had heard nothing yet, no hints at all.

Alex pulled up outside Quinn's house. Quinn slid into the seat next to Alex. The LaCrosse sedan cruised effortlessly over the hilly city streets. They turned onto Bigelow Boulevard. Alex sucked in his breath sharply. It hadn't occurred to him that the route between Quinn's house and the warehouse would take them right past the location of his accident.

Stopped at a traffic light, Alex studied the spot where his car had rolled and where it had come to rest. Nothing from the accident remained—no black streaks on the curb, no shattered glass.

"This is it," he said softly. Quinn glanced at him quizzically. "This is where my second chance started."

"Your accident was here?" Quinn asked.

"Right over there," Alex pointed. "My life was turned upside down here. In a way, I actually started coming home after that."

The light turned green, and Alex lifted his foot off the brake, starting slowly. A car behind him honked.

"You know, Quinn—in that moment I prayed. God and I were definitely not on regular speaking terms."

Quinn said, "You should pick that conversation back up. I recommend it."

When they arrived at the East Liberty warehouse, Alex took his time treading over the rocky driveway, and Quinn stepped ahead to open the door. Alex stood in the doorway of the dark building, remembering what had happened here. The excitement of aligning and committing to a Greater Goal came rushing back. It was satisfying to think about. On that day, he had been a giver.

He could hear the sharp clack-clack of Quinn's shoes on the concrete floor and wondered where the lights were. Then there was a click, and the lights came up slowly. There in silence, more than three hundred people stood before him. Kevin Jordan walked forward alone, slowly beginning to clap. Quinn joined him and also began to clap. Alex was too stunned to speak. The senior team and the board stepped forward next and joined in.

With that, the others from throughout Beckley stepped forward and joined the rising applause. Alex spotted John J. Williams in the crowd, wearing the lab coat and nametag of a newly hired research assistant. He saw his mom beaming and in tears. Rachel came running through the crowd right to him.

He hoisted her up and held her. Above the crowd was a simple banner: "Welcome Home Alex, our CEO."

He felt so loved, so humbled, and so much among family. Quinn leaned close and whispered to him, "Alex, your dad would be so proud of you." His hands fell on Alex's shoulders in a father's embrace.

"Well done."

THE END—AND A NEW BEGINNING

Five Practices for Greater Goal and Shared Goal Achievement

Practice One: Commit to the Greater Goal
- Your Greater Goal is not about you.
- The power comes from full alignment to the Greater Goal.

Practice Two: Construct Shared Goals
- Real teamwork is enabled by shared goals.
- Shared goal achievement is in turn enabled by shared leadership.

Practice Three: Cascade Greater Goal Coaching
- Aim for breakthroughs.
- Build bridges and break through barriers.
- Build on strengths, assets, and success.
- Create learning teams and be a thinking partner.

Practice Four: Reinforce Alignment
- Radical commitment is reserved for what we treasure.
- Alignment is opposed by mostly invisible forces. Make them visible and defeat them.

Practice Five: Build on Success
- Search for what's working and scale it up.
- Create a culture of innovation in pursuit of the Greater Goal.

Special Thanks

This book, like a living river, has many tributaries. Our ThirdRiver team and many great clients allowed us to put these ideas into practice and then write about the results. Renee Aukeman Prymus helped make our first drafts of ideas and stories greater. She is a gifted writer and will have many more book projects in her future. Abby Straus used her artistic skill to bring our stars and little people to life. John Porcari added Greater Goal Coaching and an unwavering belief in the purpose-performance connection. Amy Foster embodies belief in our business and in a life lived for Greater Goals. Melissa Feeney and Christina Ballard keep our back office and hospitality afloat. Sara Jennings, Lexi Joachim, and Matt Jennings were always there for us as Greater Goal advocates—they give us confidence in the future. Lee Scott contributed encouragement and a pair of cleats. Our consulting colleagues have taught us the joys and challenges of collaborating, and we will always be grateful for the lessons learned.

For consultants, nothing great happens without a great client, and our clients are awesome and often courageous. (And none of them would think of themselves that way, which is part of what makes them our favorite serving leaders.) Joe Patrnchak added encouragement and modeled wholehearted alignment to a Greater Goal. Dan Bradbury proves that these ideas can work in a world-class company and that values matter. Newt Crenshaw showed us how to lead and to make a difference in the world, while facing life's most difficult circumstances, and never waver in his care for his friends and family. These are among the greats.

Being supporters of Berrett-Koehler and the BK Authors Coop and their Greater Goal of creating *a world that works for all* has been one of life's most satisfying gifts. We have been supported by our faith community and have amazing friends at Lead Like Jesus, Renovare, Twelve Stones Ministries, and our church, The Open Door. We labor alongside friends. The blessings never stop.

About the Authors

Ken Jennings is a recognized expert and trusted advisor in organizational effectiveness and counsels senior leadership teams on mission-critical projects while helping them build collaborative leadership skills. Also a popular seminar and conference speaker, Ken gives practical advice on achieving strategic breakthroughs through focusing on Greater Goals, shared goal achievement, and Greater Goal Coaching for teams and individuals.

At the heart of Ken's leadership philosophy is a passion for "putting servant leadership to work." His best-selling book, *The Serving Leader: 5 Powerful Actions That Will Transform Your Team, Your Business, and Your Community*, coauthored with John Stahl-Wert, was published in the Ken Blanchard leadership series. This book centers on leading with integrity and purpose.

Drawing on a background of consulting across all major industries, with experience in life sciences and healthcare delivery, Ken works at many healthcare technology, pharmaceutical, and biotechnology organizations, as well as at over twenty-five academic medical centers and integrated delivery systems. With his partner and wife, Heather Hyde, Ken founded ThirdRiver Partners, which is committed to bringing world-class consulting services to great leaders and institutions.

Ken is a past codirector of the Global Leadership in Healthcare Program at the University of Michigan Business School, where he engaged clients in intensive action-learning projects to deliver leadership and team development while accomplishing critical strategic project goals. He was also a global managing partner at Accenture in health care and change management. He led engagements in strategic planning, postmerger integration, disease and medical management, e-commerce, organizational transformation, and team development.

Ken holds a doctorate in organizational development from Purdue University, a master of science in management from the Air Force Institute of Technology, and a bachelor of science in behavioral science from the Air Force Academy. He is also a graduate of the Kellogg Management Institute at Northwestern University. A respected author, Ken's early work included innovative solutions for the healthcare industry that are widely implemented today. *Changing Health Care: Creating Tomorrow's Winning Health Enterprise Today* focused on the key strategies and core competencies used by leading health organizations to transform health care.

Ken's other faculty experience includes positions as adjunct professor in leadership at Columbia University Business School; adjunct professor in strategy and leadership at Wheaton College; strategy lecturer at King's Fund College in London; faculty in management at the University of Maryland, East Asian Division; fellowship faculty at the American

College of Healthcare Executives; graduate faculty in organizational behavior at the Air Force Institute of Technology; and Visiting Scholar at Shanghai University of Finance and Economics.

Ken Jennings can be reached at Ken@3rd-River.com.

 Heather Hyde consults with ThirdRiver clients who are engaged in strategy execution and leadership development initiatives. Most important to Heather is to work with leaders to create ownership at the individual level through commitments that are relevant, transparent, and compelling. She has acted as a trusted advisor to performance teams that have produced exceptional outcomes and is currently involved in facilitating teams focused on diverse opportunities, such as performance management and new product development.

Heather believes we have each been created with very specific gifts to offer, and through offering our gifts in the service of others, we have the potential to change our world. Her passion is to help leaders find how their special gifts and strengths can be energized and engaged to achieve Greater Goals in service to a world that works for all. Heather loves to bring new perspectives to conference audiences and is a warm and engaging speaker and a dynamic workshop facilitator.

Heather facilitates Serving Leader Team Development and Greater Goal Venture Teams. Her approach applies human performance improvement technologies to the design of learning experiences for high-performance leadership teams. She draws on a background in strategic planning that begins with understanding how value is created. She works with management to create ownership at the individual level of goals that are relevant and valued.

Heather developed expertise consulting in a wide variety of public- and private-sector organizations. She was active in turnaround and crisis management in her early career as a certified public accountant and certified insolvency and reorganization advisor, developing solutions for companies in highly challenged circumstances. Following graduate work in the University of Michigan's Human Performance Improvement program, her process has been to apply rigorous analysis and review of systems affecting individuals, processes, management policies, and work environments.

Heather lives in Pittsburgh, Pennsylvania, and keeps a loving watch over her husband, Ken Jennings, and four grown children, who keep the Jenningses very busy following their exploits around the world.

Heather Hyde can be reached at Heather@3rd-River.com.

Ken and Heather invite **you** to join
the Greater Goal Community!

To view worksheets and other resources,
and to join our community, come to
http://www.TheGreaterGoal.com.

Adventures with ThirdRiver Partners

The Shared Goal Achievement™ Experience—
a Workshop for Creating Greater Goals

In this powerful day and a half experience where teams take a deep dive into the concepts, tools, and methods that drive engagement and build capability for strategy execution, you'll see results by

- Aligning individuals and teams to Greater Goals
- Growing skills in strategy execution and change management
- Building successes on breakthrough innovations
- Getting everybody connected and engaged
- Building bridges to key stakeholders

The Shared Goal Achievement™ Experience brings leaders and their teams into an intensive, interactive learning environment that accelerates the development of their capability to execute critical strategies. To increase organizational effectiveness, you will learn to

- Clarify what matters most and affirm critical team strategies
- Identify untapped strengths and possibilities to advance
- Confirm commitments and refresh specific action plans
- Recognize progress, new opportunities, and contributions to success

Enterprise success requires coordinated action toward Greater Goals. The critical strategies of multiple teams and individuals must intersect and align effectively. We will help you achieve this goal.

Shared Goal Achievement™ is a strategy-execution framework that translates critical strategic goals into powerful breakthroughs at every level of the organization. This framework

- Produces strategies that enable people to achieve Greater Goals
- Creates clear, coherent action plans that align and leverage multiple strategies, goals, and tactics
- Assigns the best talent to breakthrough opportunities
- Builds wholehearted commitment from individuals and teams whose goals and strengths are aligned with those of the organization
- Creates an environment of authentic service and value for all stakeholders

Organizations aligned in this way consistently outperform those that are not.

Ken Jennings will challenge your team with leading-edge ideas, strategies, and practical actions. Get ready for a unique and exciting experience!

—William Sterling, Chairman and Chief Executive Officer
  Trilogy Global Advisors

Serving Leader Certification—a Shared Leadership Approach

The Serving Leader Certification process enables your organization to build internal capacity and to put servant leadership to work in your organization by offering a comprehensive whole-systems change approach focused on evidence-based research and best practices. These practices include

- Facilitating shared leadership through creative dialogue
- Enhancing accountability and coordination of effort through commitment management
- Engaging in continuous improvement and practical innovation through after-action reviews
- Developing outstanding coaching capability
- Creating breakthroughs by helping employees close the gap between desired outcomes and current reality

The Certification process is focused around the Serving Leader Toolkit™, an integrated development suite of practices that allows internal coaches, facilitators, and business partners to custom design interventions for leader, team, and organizational development by mixing and matching worksheets while enabling a consistent message, language, and set of practices to proliferate throughout the organization.

Certification is delivered through an action-learning process that focuses on direct application both individually and collectively and enables participants to start to cascade and integrate Serving Leader practices throughout the organization while learning the material. Peer and expert feedback, intervention coaching, and observation are integrated into the certification process.

 ### Greater Goal Coaching™—a Uniquely Powerful Discipline to Achieve Shared Goals

Every interaction a leader has offers an opportunity to positively influence the performance of the organization. ThirdRiver Partners' Greater Goal Coaching™ approach uniquely equips your leaders to coach and collaborate with others to achieve the Greater Goals of your organization.

Those who experience Greater Goal Coaching™ will

- Capitalize on successful breakthroughs as they occur, building bridges to key stakeholders and fearlessly confronting barriers that arise
- Create powerful teams that employ the deep strengths of their members by leveraging key organizational assets and successes
- Build dynamic learning teams who proactively diagnose the reasons for success and failure, make critical adjustments, and continually innovate to create new competitive advantages

Also by Ken Jennings, with John Stahl-Wert

The Serving Leader
5 Powerful Actions That Will Transform Your Team, Your Business, and Your Community
Foreword by Ken Blanchard

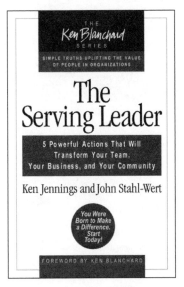

The Serving Leader makes the case for a new kind of business leadership, based on a moral code, more effective than the traditional approach. Serving leaders are qualified to be first by putting other people first. Ken Jennings and John Stahl-Wert explain this paradox, outlining the basics of servant leadership in this business fable. Telling the story about an estranged son, his dying father, and a remarkable group of innovative leaders, the authors illustrate five key principles of servant leadership. This is the most practical servant leadership guide available, as well as a tale about the personal journey of growth that real leadership requires.

Paperback, 144 pages, ISBN 978-1-57675-308-8
PDF ebook, ISBN 978-1-60994-205-2

BK® Berrett–Koehler Publishers, Inc.
San Francisco, *www.bkconnection.com*   **800.929.2929**

Berrett–Koehler
Publishers

Berrett-Koehler is an independent publisher dedicated to an ambitious mission: *Creating a World That Works for All*.

We believe that to truly create a better world, action is needed at all levels—individual, organizational, and societal. At the individual level, our publications help people align their lives with their values and with their aspirations for a better world. At the organizational level, our publications promote progressive leadership and management practices, socially responsible approaches to business, and humane and effective organizations. At the societal level, our publications advance social and economic justice, shared prosperity, sustainability, and new solutions to national and global issues.

A major theme of our publications is "Opening Up New Space." Berrett-Koehler titles challenge conventional thinking, introduce new ideas, and foster positive change. Their common quest is changing the underlying beliefs, mindsets, institutions, and structures that keep generating the same cycles of problems, no matter who our leaders are or what improvement programs we adopt.

We strive to practice what we preach—to operate our publishing company in line with the ideas in our books. At the core of our approach is stewardship, which we define as a deep sense of responsibility to administer the company for the benefit of all of our "stakeholder" groups: authors, customers, employees, investors, service providers, and the communities and environment around us.

We are grateful to the thousands of readers, authors, and other friends of the company who consider themselves to be part of the "BK Community." We hope that you, too, will join us in our mission.

A BK Business Book

This book is part of our BK Business series. BK Business titles pioneer new and progressive leadership and management practices in all types of public, private, and nonprofit organizations. They promote socially responsible approaches to business, innovative organizational change methods, and more humane and effective organizations.

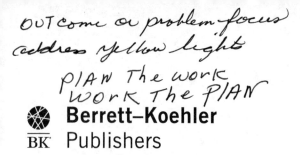

Out come or problem focus address yellow lights

Plan the work work the plan

Berrett–Koehler
Publishers

A community dedicated to creating
a world that works for all

Visit Our Website: www.bkconnection.com

Read book excerpts, see author videos and Internet movies, read
our authors' blogs, join discussion groups, download book apps, find
out about the BK Affiliate Network, browse subject-area libraries of
books, get special discounts, and more!

Subscribe to Our Free E-Newsletter, the *BK Communiqué*

Be the first to hear about new publications, special discount offers,
exclusive articles, news about bestsellers, and more! Get on the list
for our free e-newsletter by going to **www.bkconnection.com**.

Get Quantity Discounts

Berrett-Koehler books are available at quantity discounts for orders
of ten or more copies. Please call us toll-free at (800) 929-2929 or
email us at bkp.orders@aidcvt.com.

Join the BK Community

BKcommunity.com is a virtual meeting place where people from
around the world can engage with kindred spirits to create a world
that works for all. BKcommunity.com members may create their own
profiles, blog, start and participate in forums and discussion groups,
post photos and videos, answer surveys, announce and register for
upcoming events, and chat with others online in real time. Please join
the conversation!

What is the higher purpose of your work and how lives are changed for the better